EDINBURGH

Everyman MapGuides

Welcome to Edinburgh!

This opening fold-out contains a general map of Edinburgh to help you visualise the 6 large districts discussed in this guide, and 4 pages of valuable information, handy tips and useful addresses.

Discover Edinburgh through 6 district

A Edinburgh Castle / Old Town Wes

G000240762

B Old Town East / Calton Hill
C New Town
D Holyrood / Arthur's Seat
E West Edinburgh
F Leith / Portobello

For each district there is a double-page of addresses (restaurants – listed in ascending order of price – cafés, bars, tearooms and shops), followed by a fold-out map for the relevant area with the essential places to see (indicated on the map by a star ★). These places are by no means all that Edinburgh has to offer, but to us they are unmissable. The grid-referencing system (**A** B2) makes it easy for you to pinpoint addresses quickly on the map.

Transportation and hotels in Edinburgh

The last fold-out consists of a transportation map and 4 pages of practical information that include a selection of hotels.

Thematic index

Lists all the street names, sites and monuments featured in this guide.

FESTIVAL VENUES

Map labels:
DEAN GARDENS · QUEEN STREET GARDENS · Greenside Place · THE EDINBURGH PLAYHOUSE · REGENT GARDENS · CALTON · Charlotte Square · BOOK FESTIVAL · EAST PRINCES STREET GARDENS · TOURIST INFORMATION CENTRE · CANONGATE · THE ROSS THEATRE · Princes St. · HAWTHORNDEN LECTURE THEATRE · WEST PRINCES STREET GARDENS · TATTOO BOX OFFICE · FRINGE BOX OFFICE · WEST END · Lothian Rd · THE HUB · USHER HALL · TRAVERSE THEATRE · ROYAL MUSEUM · LECTURE THEATRE · FILM FESTIVAL BOX OFFICE · ROYAL LYCEUM THEATRE · OLD TOWN · Grindlay Street · EDINBURGH FESTIVAL THEATRE · DUMBIEDYKES · Nicholson Street · Lothian Street · Clerk Street · KING'S THEATRE · Leven Street · THE MEADOWS · BRUNTSFIELD LINKS · THE QUEEN'S HALL

April

International Science Festival (ten days, early April).
www.sciencefestival.co.uk

May

Scottish International Children's Festival (last week). Britain's biggest festival of performing arts for children.
www.imaginate.org.uk

June

Be prepared for midges! They infest the Highlands and Islands in summer, thriving in dampness and shade.
Caledonian Beer Festival (first weekend). Held in the Caledonian Brewery in Slateford Road.
Tel. (0131) 337 1286
www.caledonian-brewery.co.uk

August-September

Summer in Edinburgh is a non-stop spectacular cultural showcase.
International Festival and **The Fringe** (*see* box above, right).

International Jazz & Blues Festival (ten days, end July-early Aug) in various venues.
www.jazzmusic.co.uk
International Book Festival (two weeks, Aug). Edinburgh was recently named UNESCO's first City of Literature. This is the world's largest book festival and is held in Charlotte Square Gardens.
www.edbookfest.co.uk.
Edinburgh Military Tattoo (first three weeks, Aug). Nothing to do with skin decoration: 'tattoo' comes from the closing-time cry in the inns in the Low Countries during the 17th and 18th centuries – *Doe den tap toe* ('Turn off the taps'). Military marching bands with pipes and drums players, acrobats, etc., on the Castle esplanade.
www.edinburgh-tattoo.co.uk.

International Film Festival (two weeks, Aug).
www.edfilmfest.org.uk

September

Fireworks Display (on the last day of the Festival).
Open Day: your chance to get inside some of the historic buildings in the Old Town and elsewhere in the City. You can visit 20 properties in the Old Town, including Old College, the City Chambers, the Bank of Scotland, South Bridge Vaults, the Signet Library and Old Moray House, as well as many more in the New Town and elsewhere in the city.
Mela Festival: Scotland's biggest intercultural festival, with two days celebrating Asian culture in Pilrig Park.
www.edinburgh-mela.co.uk

October

Scottish Storytelling Festival (within Scotland)
→ *Tel. (0131) 557 5724*

EDINBURGH FESTIVAL

What we refer to as the Edinburgh Festival is in fact a series of festivals. The two crowd-pullers, however, are: The **Edinburgh International Festival** (mid Aug-early Sep) and the **Fringe** (early Aug-end Aug). Founded in 1947, the EIF has earned its reputation as one of the world's greatest celebrations of performing arts, and brings to Edinburgh some of the best international dance, theatrical, musical and operatic works. The 2004 Festival saw over 160 performances of 85 different productions and concerts, with three world premieres.

The **Fringe** was born out of unofficial performances and is now enormously popular. More than 1,500 shows (amateurs or professionals) are performed in more than 300 venues. Innovative and experimental, the Fringe remains one of the best places to launch new talents. Have a taste of the Fringe on the second Sunday, as free performances are given in the Meadows.
www.edfringe.com

How to book:
→ The Hub, Castlehill
Tel. (0131) 473 2000
boxoffice@eif.co.uk
www.thehub-edinburgh.com or *www.eif.co.uk*

Most festival venues are in or very near the city center, and can be reached easily on foot. (see map above left)

PIPERS

DAVID HUME IN LAWNMARKET

GREYFRIARS BOBBY

CHRONOLOGY

1000–6000 BC: first settlers arrive in Scotland **c.800 BC:** Edinburgh Rock settled **AD 150:** Romans build Antonine Wall to mark limit of their empire **c.AD 400:** Christian missionaries arrive from Ireland **AD 500:** Scots invade from Ireland **1707:** Union of Scotland and England **1720s–90s:** David Hume, Adam Smith and others create Scottish Enlightenment **1745–6:** Jacobite Rebellion **1760s–1810s:** creation of the city's 'New Town'; dubbed 'Athens of the North' **2002:** Devolved Scottish Parliament opens

PROFILE

■ Capital of Scotland and a World Heritage Site ■ 460,000 inhabitants ■ 100 sq miles ■ 2 million visitors a year, half of which come during the Festival ■ An average of 1,351 hours of bright sunshine a year

OUTSIDE JENNERS

TOURIST INFO

Tourist offices
www.edinburgh.org
www.visitscotland.com
Edinburgh and Scotland Tourist Information Center
→ *3 Princes Street*
Tel. 0845 22 55 121 or + 44 1506 832 121 *(outside UK)*
Mon-Sat 9am–6pm; Sun 10am–6pm (8pm in summer, 5pm in winter)
Airport Information Center
→ *Tel. 0131 473 3800*
Other useful websites
→ *travelscotland.co.uk*
→ *edinburghguide.com*
→ *explore-edinburgh. com*
→ *edinburgharchitecture.co.uk*
→ *cockburnassociation.org.uk*
→ *edinburgh-festivals.com*
→ *edinburgholdtown.org.uk*
Many of Scotland's historic sites are managed by two organizations: **Historic Scotland** and the **National Trust for Scotland**
www.historic-scotland.gov.uk
www.nts.org.uk

Consulates
American Consulate General (D B1)
→ *3 Regent Terrace, Calton Hill* Tel. *(0131) 556 8315 or (0122) 4857097 (after hours emergency only)*
www.usembassy.org.uk/ scotland
Australian Consulate (C C5)
→ *69 George St, New Town* Tel. *(0131) 624 3333 (call ahead for opening times)*
Canadian Consulate (C B6)
→ *30 Lothian Rd*
Tel. *(0131) 220 4333*
Health
Royal Infirmary of Edinburgh *(south of* **D** *B4)*
→ *51 Little France Crescent*
24-hour casualty department.
Emergency Dental Institute
→ *Lauriston Building, Lauriston Place, South Edinburgh*
Tel. *(0131) 536 4955*
Mon-Fri 9am–3pm
Walk-in emergency clinic.

Boots the Chemist
→ *46 Shandwick Place and 101 Princes St*
Mon-Sat 8am–8pm (6pm Sat); Sun 10.30am–4.30pm
Left luggage
It is possible to leave your luggage at Edinburgh Airport (Departure Hall), and you'll also find lockers at St Andrew Sq bus station or Waverley Station.

USEFUL NUMBERS

Dialing codes
Calling Edinburgh from the US
→ *011 + 44 (UK) + 131 (city code) + 7-digit number*
Calling abroad from Edinburgh
→ *00 + country code (1 for USA and Canada) + number*
Calls within Edinburgh
→ *Omit (0131); simply dial the 7-digit number*
Calls from Edinburgh to the rest of the UK
→ *Dial the city code*

(including the 0) + number
Emergency
Police, fire, ambulance
→ *Tel. 999 (or 112 from your cellphone)*
Directory enquiries
→ *118500 or 118118 national*
→ *118505 international*
Operator
→ *100 national*
→ *155 international*

PUBLIC HOLIDAYS

(In Edinburgh) **Jan 1-2:** New Year's Day and day after. **March/April:** Good Friday and Easter Monday. **May Day:** (first Mon in May). **Victoria Day:** (last Mon in May). **August Bank Holiday:** (last Mon in Aug). **Autumn Holiday:** (third Mon in Sep). **Dec 25–26:** Christmas and Boxing Day.

DIARY OF EVENTS

January
Burns Night (Jan 25)

Welcome to Edinburgh!

A Edinburgh castle / Old Town West
B Old Town East / Calton Hill
C New Town

D Holyrood / Arthur's Seat
E Edinburgh West
F Leith / Portobello

F

NEWHAVEN HERITAGE MUSEUM

GRANTON HARBOUR

GRANTON

LOWER GRANTON ROAD (A901)

STARBANK ROAD

NEWHAVEN

LOMOND PARK

VICTORIA PARK

FERRY

PILTON

PILTON PARK

FERRY ROAD (A902)

WARRISTON

GRANTON ROAD (A903)

FERRY ROAD (A902)

FERRY ROAD

FERRY ROAD (A901)

C

INVERLEITH ROW

TELFORD ROAD (A901)

INVERLEITH PARK

ROYAL BOTANIC GARDEN

BROUGHTON

BROUGHTON RD

WATER OF LEITH

EYRE PL.

BELLEVUE

COMELY BANK

HAMILTON PL.

RAEBURN PL.

STOCKBRIDGE

SCOTTISH NATIONAL PORTRAIT GALLERY

CRAIGLEITH ROAD

COMELY BANK

ORCHARD BRAE

DEAN GARDENS

QUEEN STREET GARDENS

E

QUEENSFERRY ROAD

QUEENSFERRY ROAD

DEAN VILLAGE

A

PRINCES STREET

EDINBURGH WAVERLEY STATION

SCOTTISH NATIONAL GALLERY MODERN ART

ST MARY'S EPISCOPAL CATHEDRAL

WEST PRINCES STREET GARDENS

SHANDWICK PLACE

LOTHIAN RD (A700)

EDINBURGH CASTLE

ST GILES' CATHEDRAL

WATER OF LEITH

COATES

OLD TOWN

ROSEBURN TER.

WEST COATES

HAYMARKET TER.

MORRISON ST

HAYMARKET STATION

THE MEADOWS

MURRAYFIELD RUGBY STADIUM

DALRY

DALRY ROAD (A70)

LEAMINGTON LIFT BRIDGE

MELVILLE DRIVE (A700)

BRUNTSFIELD

MARCHMONT

GORGIE ROAD

GORGIE CITY FARM

GORGIE RD

HARRISON PARK

BRUNTSFIELD PLACE (A702)

CHURCH HILL

SLATEFORD RD

SLATEFORD RD

MERCHISTON

MORNINGSIDE ROAD

GORGIE

MEGGETLAND PLAYING FIELDS

ROYAL EDINBURGH HOSPITAL

BLACKFORD HILL

ARMSTRONG'S   **THE NUTCRACKER CHRISTMAS SHOP**   **OLD TARTAN WEAVING COMPANY**

always fine puddings and a choice of coffees. The 'gallery' part houses changing exhibitions of contemporary art.

PUBS

Bow Bar (**A** C2)
→ 80 West Bow
Tel. (0131) 226 7667
Daily 11am–11.30pm
An award-winning pub with a huge selection of whiskies and superb cask-conditioned ales. It's a comfortable place with a woody, Victorian atmosphere.

Last Drop Tavern (**A** C3)
→ 74 Grassmarket
Tel. (0131) 225 4851
Daily 11am–1am
The name ghoulishly refers to the hangings that used to take place in the Grassmarket gallows opposite the pub. It is, of course, haunted – by students mainly. The food, though, is a cut above the usual pub fare.

Deacon Brodie's Tavern (**A** D2)
→ 425 Lawnmarket
Tel. (0131) 225 6531
Daily 10am–midnight (1am Fri-Sat); food is served upstairs noon–10pm
Established in 1806, this famous tavern is named after the infamous Deacon

Brodie, a worthy burgher by day and a stealthy thief by night. Brodie was the inspiration for Stevenson's Jekyll and Hyde, and was hanged in 1788 on a gallows he reputedly 'improved' himself (for others). The wine is average, but most people come for the beer and chat (ground floor) or for the food (first floor).

SHOPPING

Armstrong's (**A** C3)
→ 83 Grassmarket
(also at 66 Clerk St)
Tel. (0131) 220 5557 Mon-Sat 10am–6pm; Sun noon–6pm
www.armstrongsvintage.co.uk
An enormous vintage clothes outlet, opened in 1840, with many rather unnerving mannequins – the more recent the clothes the weirder they look. You can pick up collectors' pieces at amazing prices, and it's great fun browsing through the vintage lace and satin. The staff were once described as looking like extras either from *Grease* or from *Gone with the Wind*, but they are very helpful. Take time to pop by the much smaller Amnesty International

shop at 11 Jeffrey St – it has more great bargains.
Scotch Whisky Heritage Centre (**A** C2)
→ 354 Castlehill
Tel. (0131) 220 0441
May-Sep: daily 9.30am–6.30pm. Oct-April 10am–6pm (last tour begins 1 hr before closing)
www.whisky-heritage.co.uk
Award-winning and popular visitor attraction, where you'll learn all about whisky production. There's a 'Ghostfest' in May for those who prefer other spirits.
The Cashmere Store of Scotland (**A** D2)
→ 2 St Giles St, Royal Mile (and 67 George St)
Tel. (0131) 225 5178
Mon-Sat 10am–5.30pm
www.scottish-cashmere.com
High-quality, traditional-style Scottish clothes. They'll make charming gifts for your aunts rather than your nieces, and the male interest is likely to be from golfers, but you won't go too far wrong buying here. Watch for special promotions, often with large price discounts.
Edinburgh Old Town Weaving Company (**A** C2)
→ 555 Castlehill
Tel. (0131) 226 4162
Mon-Sat 9am–6.30pm;

Sun 10am–5.30pm
www.geoffreykilts.co.uk
One of the few places you can watch tartan being woven. The cloth woven here is then made into kilts by the sister shop at 55–57 High St (this is where Charlton Heston and Mel Gibson get theirs).
The Old Town Bookshop (**A** D2)
→ 8 Victoria St
Tel. (0131) 225 9237
Mon-Sat 10.30am–5.45pm
www.oldtownbookshop.com
Edinburgh has many fine antiquarian bookshops such as this. The Old Town Bookshop carries a huge stock of quality second-hand books: from Renaissance folios to modern first editions.
The Nutcracker Christmas Shop (**A** D2)
→ 52 High St
Tel. (0131) 558 8228
Daily 10am–6pm
One of the spookiest shops you'll ever go into, particularly in summer. Here it is Christmas all year round, and you can buy absolutely anything to do with Christmas once beyond its portals – even, one suspects, sanity clauses. They have four other outlets, though none at the North Pole.

OUTLOOK TOWER

MAGDALEN CHAPEL

OLD TOWN

GEORGE SQUARE

GEORGE IV BRIDGE

CHALMERS ST

CHAR ST

REID CONCERT HALL & MUS.

MEADOW WALK

ARCHIBALD PL

LAURISTON PLACE

EDINBURGH DENTAL INSTITUTE

KEIR ST

HERIOT PL

TEVIOT PL

OLD COLLEGE

FORREST ROAD

FORREST HILL

BRISTO PL

BRIS PORT

★ GEORGE HERIOT'S SCHOOL

GREYFRIARS KIRK

GREYFRIARS PL

MUSEUM OF SCOTLAND & ROYAL MUSEUM OF SCOTLAND

CHAMBERS ST

AIRDS CL

HERIOT BRIDGE

GRASSMARKET

★ GRASSMARKET

WAR CANDLEMAKER ROW

CANDLEMAKER ROW

W BOW

COWGATE

VICTORIA ST

MAGDALEN CHAPEL ★

THE HUB ★

TERRACE

ESPLANADE CASTLEHILL

OUTLOOK TOWER ★

GLADSTONE'S LAND ★

LAWNMARKET ★

WRITERS' MUSEUM ★

RAMSAY GDN

GEORGE IV BRIDGE

COWGATE

LAW COURTS

PARLIAMENT HOUSE

OLD FISHMARKET CL

PARLIAMENT SQUARE

ST GILES' CATHEDRAL

BANK ST

MARY KING'S CLOSE

GILES' ST

HIGH STREET

CITY CHAMBERS

MOUND PL NORTH BK ST

COCKBURN ST

MARKET STREET

MARKET STREET

NATIONAL GALLERY OF SCOTLAND

THE MOUND

ROYAL SCOTTISH ACADEMY

EAST PRINCES ST GDNS

SCOTT MONUMENT

EDINBURGH WAVERLEY STATION

WAVERLEY BRIDGE

TOURIST INFORMATION CENTRE

PRINCES STREET

PRINCES STREET

HANOVER ST

ST DAVID'S ST

MEUSE LA.

N LANE

STREET S LANE

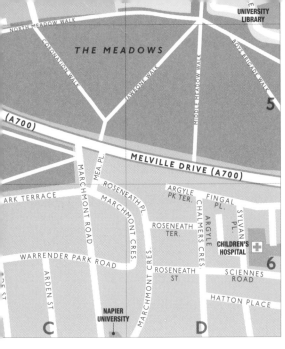

GEORGE HERIOT'S SCHOOL

GRASSMARKET

al's activity, housing stival's ticket office formation center.

rs' Museum (**A** D2)
y Stair's Close, Lawn-
. Tel. (0131) 529 4901
at 10am–5pm; Sun
during the Festival
f the oldest buildings
nburgh, Lady Stair's
contains evocative
rabilia of Scotland's
greatest writers:
Burns, Sir Walter
and R. L. Stevenson.

riars Kirk (**A** D3)
yfriars Place
31) 226 5429
reyfriarskirk.com
urgh's first post-
nation church (1620)

includes a highly atmospheric graveyard where lie architects John and Robert Adam, poet Allan Ramsay and many 17th-century monuments. Close by in Candlemakers Row is the statue of the world's most famous skye terrier, Greyfriars Bobby, who reputedly lies near to his master's grave.

Magdalen Chapel (**A** D2-3)
→ 41 Cowgate
Daily 9.30am–4.30pm
Dating from 1541, Magdalen Chapel is especially worth a visit to see the only stained glass in a Scottish church to survive the Reformation. Often a place of turmoil in

the past, the chapel is now a contemplative refuge.

Grassmarket (**A** C3)
Formerly the site of a cattle market (15th–20th c.), a place of public execution (18th c.) immortalised in Scott's *Heart of Midlothian*, and once the haunt of bodysnatchers Burke and Hare, the Grassmarket is today a square popular with students and locals, with great shops and cafés.

George Heriot's School (**A** C3)
→ Lauriston Place
George Heriot's, opened in 1659 for 'poor boys' and now one of the most exclusive schools in the

country, is closed to the public; but you can view the quadrangle and admire the architecture – perhaps the most imposing the Scottish Renaissance has to offer.

Usher Hall (**A** C3)
→ Lothian Road
Tel. (0131) 221 6332
www.usherhall.co.uk
Flanked by two of the city's great theaters, the Royal Lyceum and the Traverse, the Usher Hall is well known for its magnificent dome, but it is almost equally impressive inside. Funded by the philanthropist Andrew Usher and finished in 1914, this is one of the world's great concert halls.

ST GILES' CATHEDRAL

MARY KING'S CLOSE

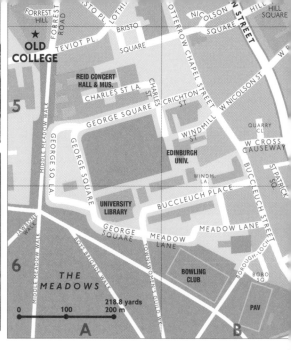

Parliament Square (B A3)

The greatest public square in Scotland saw many public executions and the return from exile of Mary, Queen of Scots. Behind St Giles is a 19th-century replica of the Mercat Cross, where public proclamations were read. Behind St Giles by the 19th-century replica of the Mercat Cross, where public proclamations were traditionally read, is the 'Heart of Midlothian', patterned in stone and onto which locals still spit for good luck.

Parliament House (B A3)

→ Parliament Square
Galleries open to the public
Mon-Fri 9am–5pm
Now the hub of the Scottish legal system, this building was founded in the 1630s to house the Scottish Parliament – a function it filled until 1707. See the stunning 17th-century main hall with its hammer-beam roof and watch Scotland's senior legal minds at work.

St Giles' Cathedral (B A3)

→ Royal Mile
Tel. (0131) 226 2998
Mon-Fri 9am–7pm (5pm Oct-April); Sat 9am–5pm; Sun 1–5pm. www.stgiles.net
Seen as the mother church of world presbyterianism, the High Kirk of St Giles is commonly referred to as a cathedral, but it was only a bishop's seat for 23 years out of its 1,000 of existence.

It began life as a small 9th-century parish church, officially dedicated in 1243. Substantially altered in the 15th century (the crown spire was finished in 1495) and restored in the 19th, the church is drenched in Scottish history.

Museum of Scotland & Royal Museum (B A4)

→ Chambers St
Tel. (0131) 247 4422 (M of S)
Tel. (0131) 247 4219 (RM)
Mon-Sat 10am–5pm (8pm Tue); Sun noon–5pm
www.nms.ac.uk
The **Museum of Scotland**'s aim is to present 'the story of Scotland (its land, people and culture) through the rich national collections. Though

the layout is a bit confu
it succeeds in those ter
The building itself (199
a modern gem in golde
sandstone. The collecti
the ambitious **Royal Mu**
cover the Natural World
(minerals, evolution,
fossils...), , Science and
Industry, and Decorativ
(Ancient Egypt, Islam, C
Japan...).

Old College (B A5)

→ South Bridge
Robert Adam designed
plans for the stunning
Edinburgh University C
College, but his death i
1792 and then lack of f
meant that the building
only completed in 1834
William Playfair. The

THE ROYAL MUSEUM

OLD COLLEGE

MUSEUM OF SCOTLAND

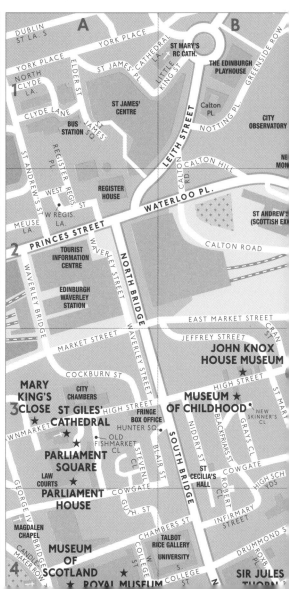

A

B

DUBLIN ST LA. S

YORK PLACE

ST JAMES' CATHEDRAL

ST MARY'S RC CATH.

LITTLE KING ST

THE EDINBURGH PLAYHOUSE

GREENSIDE ROW

YORK PLACE

ST JAMES' PL.

NORTH CLYDE LA.

1

ELDER ST

CLYDE LANE

ST JAMES' CENTRE

Calton Pl.

CITY OBSERVATORY

NOTTING PL.

NE MON

BUS STATION

ST JAMES SQ.

LEITH STREET

CALTON HILL

ST ANDREW'S ST

REGISTER PL.

WEST REGIS. ST

REGISTER HOUSE

CALTON RD.

WATERLOO PL.

MEUSE LA.

W REGIS. LA.

ST ANDREW'S (SCOTTISH EX

PRINCES STREET

2

WAVERLEY BRIDGE

TOURIST INFORMATION CENTRE

WAVERLEY STREET

NORTH BRIDGE

CALTON ROAD

EDINBURGH WAVERLEY STATION

EAST MARKET STREET

MARKET STREET

WAVERLEY STREET

JEFFREY STREET

CRAN ST

JOHN KNOX HOUSE MUSEUM ★

COCKBURN ST

HIGH STREET

ST MARY

MARY KING'S CLOSE ★

CITY CHAMBERS

ST GILES' CATHEDRAL ★

HIGH STREET

FRINGE BOX OFFICE

MUSEUM OF CHILDHOOD ★

NEW SKINNER'S CL

3

WNMARKET

★

HUNTER SQ.

BLACKFRIARS ST

GRAYS CL

OLD FISHMARKET CL

NIDDRY ST

PARLIAMENT SQUARE ★

STEVENL. CL

BLAIR ST

SOUTH BRIDGE

COWGATE

LAW COURTS ★

ST CECILIA'S HALL

ROBERT ST

HIGH SCH YDS

PARLIAMENT HOUSE

COWGATE

GUH. ST

GEORGE IV

INFIRMARY STREET

MAGDALEN CHAPEL

CHAMBERS ST

DRUMMOND S

4

CANDLEMAKER ROW

MUSEUM OF SCOTLAND ★

TALBOT RICE GALLERY

UNIVERSITY S.

ROXB

COLLEGE ST

W. COLLEGE ST

SIR JULES THORN

★ ROYAL MUSEUM

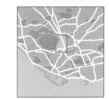

Saki could have been speaking of Edinburgh's Old Town when he said of Crete, it 'produces more history than it can consume locally'. History is all about *you* here: in St Giles' Cathedral, regarded by many presbyterians as their founding church, and in the two world-class museums in Chambers Street. A good public resting place is on one of the benches in Parliament Square, where you can watch the world and her auntie stroll and shop along the Royal Mile. Climb atop the volcanic Calton Hill where, standing by the 'Scottish Parthenon' (William PlayFair's National Monument) you will get a magnificent view of the city, even on a *dreich* (dull and wet) day.

RESTAURANTS

Creelers (B A3)
→ 3 Hunter Square
Tel. (0131) 220 4447
Mon-Sat noon–2.30pm,
5.30–10.30pm (11pm Fri-Sat);
closed for lunch Tue-Wed,
Sun 12.30–3pm, 6–10.30pm
The first Creelers opened on the Isle of Arran along with a quality smokery, and the Edinburgh branch (opened 1992) has rapidly gained a great reputation for imaginative cooking with high-quality Scottish seafood, which comes straight from the Western Isles via the smokehouse to the table. Creelers has an ethical policy with regard to sourcing fish, so you can eat their fish with a clear conscience and their mail-order service is second to none, £12–23.

David Bann (B A3)
→ 56-58 St Mary's St
Tel. (0131) 556 5888 Daily
11am–10pm (1am Fri-Sat)
www.davidbann.co.uk
David Bann pulled away at this location trailing clouds of glory from his last venture and is now threatening to become an Edinburgh institution. This may be one of the best vegetarian restaurants in Britain, and carnivores won't miss shredding the flesh when the risottos, curries and burgers are as good as they are here. £20.

Black Bo's (B B3)
→ 57-61 Blackfriars St
Tel. (0131) 557 6136
Daily 6–10.30pm (also lunch Fri-Sat noon–2pm)
Mainly vegetarian, but has a little something for the carnivores', this is a gourmet establishment with non-gourmet prices. Truly inventive without being daft, this is where Edinburgh's 'Beautiful Ones' like to eat (and drink, as Black Bo's pub is next door – a tiny, convivial bar with great bar staff). £20.

Dubh Prais (B A3)
→ 123b High St
Tel. (0131) 557 5732
Tue-Fri noon–2pm, 6.30–
10.30pm; Sat 6.30–10.30pm
Dubh Prais ('black cooking pot' in Gaelic) is a tiny, fiercely Scottish place that serves good Scottish fare and two of the best-known dishes that aren't always on the menu elsewhere: kedgeree, a mixture of cooked smoked haddock and rice (or pearl barley) in a curry sauce, and a much praised haggis. Unfussy and unpretentious, it's the perfect place to regroup amid the tartan inferno of the Royal Mile. £22.

DAVID BANN

TOWER

The Royal Mile, the tourist hub of Edinburgh, consists of four streets – Castle Hill, Lawnmarket, High street and Canongate – that trace a straight line from the Castle to the Palace of Holyroodhouse. The High Street is bordered by closes and inner courts, and its beautifully uniformed houses remind us that from 1677 it became unlawful to use building materials other than stone, slate and tiles. A visit to the Castle could consume all your time, but don't miss out on the many attractions on Castlehill and the Lawnmarket. But there are quieter places nearby to take refuge, such as Greyfriars Kirk.

Restaurant prices are based on a two-course meal for one, plus a glass of wine, excluding service.

BRODIE'S TAVERN

THE BOW BAR

RESTAURANTS

Monster Mash (A D3)
➔ 4a Forrest Road
Tel. (0131) 225 7069
Mon–Fri 8am–10pm; Sat–Sun 9am–10pm (10am Sun)
No nouvelle cuisine here! A very popular place, with a focus on classic British grub: notably (of course) bangers 'n' mash, but with a twist. The sausages are high quality and ethical (free-range pork), and they even come in a vegetarian version. Delicious gravies, too. Meal £11.

The Witchery by the Castle (A C2)
➔ 352 Castlehill
Tel. (0131) 225 5613 Daily noon–4pm, 5.30pm–11.30pm
www.thewitchery.com
The Witchery is a luxurious place to stay and a fantastic place to eat. Built in 1595 in the shadow of the castle, Andrew Lloyd Webber calls it 'the prettiest restaurant ever', which most of its patrons feel. You can practically absorb high living by just reading about this place. The two-course lunch at £12.50 is a bargain.

The Atrium (A A3)
➔ 10 Cambridge St
Tel. (0131) 228 8882
Mon–Sat noon–2pm, 6–10pm; closed Fri lunch

This is one of the best restaurants in the city. The decor is a modern mix of canvas-covered chairs, copper-rod light fittings and rough-plastered walls. The food is a serious, continuously good blend of the Scottish and Mediterranean. Interesting wines by the glass. Three-course set lunch is £17.50; set dinner, £25. Above the Atrium, to which it belongs, is the Blue Bar Café, where more reasonably priced lighter meals are served. Innovative and first-rate.

CAFÉS

Fed & Watered (A C2)
➔ 29 Grassmarket
Tel. (0131) 225 8387 Mon–Fri 8am–5pm; Sat 10am–5pm
A good refuge when you tire of the Grassmarket cobblestones. The food is tasty and fresh, and you'll be reinvigorated and back into the shops in no time.

The Fruitmarket Gallery Café (A D1)
➔ 45 Market St
Tel. (0131) 226 1843
Mon–Sat 11.30am–3.45pm, Sun noon–3.45pm (later for just coffee and cake)
www.fruitmarket.co.uk
Excellent simple food (soups are all vegetarian),

BROUGH...

LAURIST PK

LAURIST ST

GLEN ST

TOLL CROSS JUNCTION

TOLL CROSS

LAURISTON PLACE

EARL GREY ST

DUNBAR ST

4

FOUNTAINBRIDGE

PORT HAMILTON

HIGH RIGGS

WEST PORT

LADY LAWSON

LAURISTON ST

BR. ST LANE

FOUNTAINBRIDGE

SEMPLE ST

LOTHIAN ROAD (A700)

MORRISON ST

BREAD ST

CHUCKIE PEND

SPITTAL ST

GRINDLAY CT ST

GRINDLAY ST

CORNWALL ST

FILMHOUSE

3

LADY LAWSON ST

CASTLE TER

CAMBRIDGE ST

ROYAL LYCEUM

USHER HALL

ARGYLE HOUSE

KING'S STAB...

TRAVERSE THEATRE

CASTLE TERRACE

WEST APPROACH ROAD

ROYAL SCOT... MUSE...

KING'S STABLES ROAD

★ EDINBUR... CASTL...

NATIONAL WAR MUS. OF SCOTLAND

LOTHIAN ROAD (A700)

RUTLAND ST

WEST END

ROSS THEATRE

WEST PRINCES STREET GARDENS

PRINCES STREET

HOPE ST LA.

HOPE ST

FREDERICK ST

CASTLE ST

ROSE STREET LANE S

N LANE

GEORGE STREET

CASTLE ST

LANE N

LANE S

CHARLOTTE SQUARE

YOUNG ST LANE S

N CHAR... ST

CASTLE ST

YOUNG ST

LANE N

GEORGE STREET

CHARLOTTE ST

ALBERT MEMORIAL

WEST REGISTER HOUSE

GEORGIAN HOUSE

1

2

B

A

GREYFRIARS KIRK

LAWNMARKET

EDINBURGH CASTLE

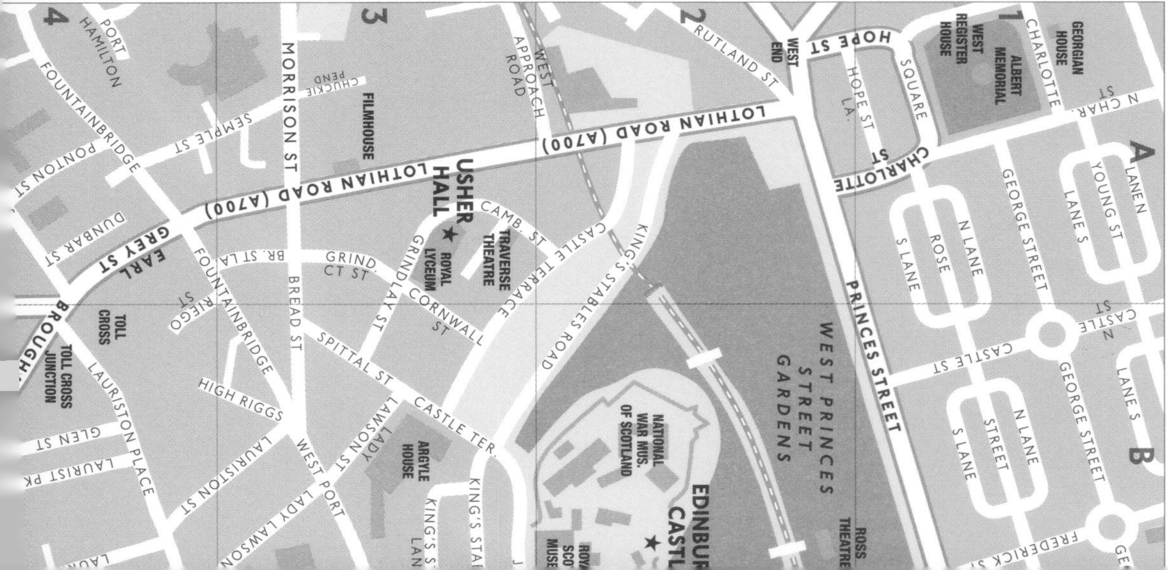

WRITERS' MUSEUM

THE HUB

218.8 yards
0   100   200 m

Edinburgh Castle (A B2)
➔ Tel. (0131) 225 9846
April-Oct: daily 9.30am–6pm,
(5pm Nov-March)
Gloriously set atop a rocky
hill (an extinct volcano),
Edinburgh Castle was the
royal residence from the 11th
century before Holyrood
Abbey was established.
A military stronghold often
besieged and the seat
of the crown jewels (the
Honours of Scotland), it is
Scotland's most popular
attraction. You could spend
several days exploring its
treasures: the Scottish
National War Memorial, the
Stone of Destiny and the
oldest of the castle's

buildings, St Margaret's
Chapel (12th c.).
Outlook Tower (A D2)
➔ Castlehill, Royal Mile
Tel. (0131) 226 3709 Daily
9.30am–6pm (later in summer)
The 17th-century tower has
housed an amazing and
world-renowned giant
camera obscura since the
1850s; photographic and
optical exhibitions with
kaleidoscopes; the world's
biggest plasma-dome; a
morphing machine; and 3-D
holograms. The telescopes
on the rooftop terrace allow
fantastic views of the city.
Lawnmarket (A D2)
The name derives from the
fine linen cloth – 'lawn' –

that was sold here until the
18th century. Apart from
Gladstone's Land and the
Writer's Museum, this area
has some of the most
haunting closes and courts
of Auld Edinburgh – the
prestigious James Court,
where the philosopher
David Hume lived and
where Boswell entertained
Dr Johnson in 1773, Milne's
Court (student residences)
and Brodie's Close, named
after the father of the
infamous Deacon Brodie.
Gladstone's Land (A D2)
➔ 477B Lawnmarket
Tel. (0131) 226 5856 April-Oct:
daily 10am–5pm (Sun 2–5pm)
The exquisite early 17th-

century mansion of Thom
Gledstanes has been
restored and refurnishe
show a taste of privilege
in old Edinburgh: the 17
century wall friezes are
stunning. You can also r
a holiday apartment.
The Hub (A C2)
➔ Castlehill, Royal Mile
Tel. (0131) 473 2010
Mon-Sat 10am–5pm
www.eif.co.uk/thehub
Built in the 1840s as an
assembly hall for the Ch
of Scotland, this striking
Victorian gothic buildin;
was co-designed by A. ▶
and has the tallest spire
Edinburgh (44 ft). It is a
main point for Edinburg

A

PRINCES STREET

PALACE OF HOLYROODHOUSE

THE CITY FROM CALTON HILL

December-January

Edinburgh's three-day New Year street party, better known as Hogmanay, is the biggest in the world (wrap up warm!). Book ahead if you want to get close to the city center's main party area on Dec 31. *www.edinburghshogmanay.org*

SHOPPING

Food
Try the chocolate, jams, marmalades (Baxters), teas, chutney, Indian and Chinese spices, Highland biscuits and shortbreads.

Antiques
Nineteenth-century craft objects, firearms, copper, pewter and silverware from the various antique markets in the main towns or from antique shops.

Barbour
Barbour is famous for its classic waterproof (waxed cotton) jackets.

Jewelry
There is some stunning silver jewelry reproducing Celtic motifs.

Knitwear
Best-quality wool and traditionally made garments. A wide range of wool-based products, including tartan and the warm and very comfortable Shetland sweaters. James Pringle and Harris Tweed are two of the most prestigious wool marks.

Pottery and glass
The items produced by the Bridge of Allen and Wick workshops (glass), and Highland Stoneware (pottery), are renowned for their balanced composition and their clean lines.

Whisky
Inimitable whiskies that are only available in Scotland. Each region has its own varieties and aromas. Buy a copy of the *Collins Whisky Map of Scotland* (£4.50).

EATING & DRINKING

Evening meals are usually eaten earlier (7.30–9.30pm) rather than later. Cheese is usually served after dessert.

Restaurants
Usually open noon–2pm and 6.30–10.30pm. Prices are often quite high. Pub meals in the lounge bar are cheaper. Reserve a table, especially in the evening.

Fast food
Fish 'n' chip shops sell takeout fish or chicken 'n' chips, and sometimes haggis at unbeatable prices.

Beer
Served by the pint (¾ US pint). A wide range of different brews – try the traditional Scottish real ales, such as Arran Blonde or Orkney Skullspitter!

Wine
In restaurants, wine can be served by the glass. As a rule, wine is pricey in the UK. Chilean, South African

SOME SCOTTISH SPECIALTIES

Scotland is second to none for its fresh ingredients, favored by today's top chefs: poached wild salmon, smoked salmon, prawns (langoustines), beef and game (grouse, venison etc.) and, of course, scottish raspberries – the best in the world.

Haggis
Made from sheep's offal mixed with beef suet and lightly toasted oatmeal, placed inside the sheep's stomach, which is then sewn closed and boiled for a few hours.

Smoked haddock
The most common white fish on offer in Scotland, under the names of 'Arbroath smokie' (wood-smoked and produced in small family-run smoke-houses in the East Coast fishing town of Arbroath) or 'Finnan haddie'.

Porridge
A simple dish usually eaten for breakfast, made of slowly boiled oatmeal, stirred continuously with the traditional spirtle (a wooden stick) to avoid the formation of lumps.

Bannocks (oatcakes)
A barley and oat-flour biscuit baked on a griddle. Today bannocks are often eaten with cheese.

Cranachan
Traditional Scotttish dessert (raspberries or strawberries), lots of cream, honey, single malt whisky, oatmeal.

RALLYING ON THE MEADOWS

PORTOBELLO PROMENADE

DRINKING ON GRASSMARKET

THE GARDENS OF THE SCOTTISH NATIONAL PORTRAIT GALLERY

and Australian wines tend to be cheaper than French wines, and just as good.

Whisky

Order a dram: a small glass blended or single malt whisky. Visit the Scotch Whisky Heritage Centre, Castlehill, Edinburgh.

SMOKING

A total ban on smoking in public places throughout Scotland is planned from Spring 2006.

ENTERTAINMENT

Cultural listings
The List, fortnightly, covers Edinburgh and Glasgow events. *www.list.co.uk*
Scotsgay, a monthly; free in gay venues. Lists gay and general events.
Theater
Royal Lyceum (A A3)
→ 30 Grindlay St
Tel. (0131) 248 4800

www.lyceum.org.uk
This glorious theater (1883) has seen most of the great stage actors. Book early as the productions here are very popular.
Edinburgh Playhouse (B B1)
→ 18-22 Greenside Place
Tel. (0131) 524 3333
Stages the big musicals and concerts from London's West End.
Festival Theatre (B B4) & **Kings Theatre (A** B5)
→ Tel. (0131) 529 6000
www.eft.co.uk
Both venues (Festival at 13 Nicolson St, Kings at 2 Leven St) put on a wide variety of shows, ranging from ballet to kid's shows.
The Traverse Theatre (A A3)
→ 10 Cambridge St
Tel. (0131) 228 1404
www.traverse.co.uk
Contemporary theater of the highest quality.
Comedy
Stand Comedy Club (B A1)
→ 5 York Place

Tel. (0131) 558 7272
Mon-Sat 7.30pm–midnight, Sun occasional lunchtime show. www.thestand.co.uk
Acts can be awful, but you may get to see a future star – who knows? Only holds 160, so phone for tickets.
Music
Liquid Room (A D2)
→ 9c Victoria St
Tel. (0131) 225 2564
Mainstream club in a subterranean vault for live music, dance and indie stuff
Usher Hall (see **E**)
Museums
Entrance fees
The City of Edinburgh museums and galleries (*www.cac.org.uk*) are free. A charge is made for exhibitions at the National Galleries of Scotland.
Opening hours
Usually open Mon-Sat 10am–5pm with a late opening Tue or Thu; Sun noon–5pm.

TOURS

Literary tours
Rebustours
Easter-end Sep on Sat-Sun. Reservation essential During the Fringe Festival in August book your tickets from www.edfringe.com or www.rebustours.com
The two very popular Rebus walking routes take in the Old and New Town, and the various places mentioned in Rankin's books.
The Macallan Edinburgh Literary Pub Tour
Tel. 08001 697 410
Learn about Scotland's literary heroes and their favorite pubs. The tour finishes in one, Milne's Bar, originally a meeting place of the Scottish literati.
Ghostly tours
Edinburgh is a city of stories and legends, and haunting characters.
Mercat Walking Tours
Tel. (0131) 557 6464
www.mercattours.com
To know all about the Royal Mile, the Old Town vaults, the haunted underground and more.
City of the Dead Tours
Tel. (0131) 225 9044
www.blackhart.uk.com
Entertaining, but can be quite scary as in one tour you get locked up at night in the Black Mausoleum – yes, one that purportedly contains the MacKenzie Poltergeist!
Bus tours
Edinburgh Tour
www.edinburghtour.com
All tours depart from Waverley Bridge. Tickets valid for 24 hrs – hop on and off as you please.

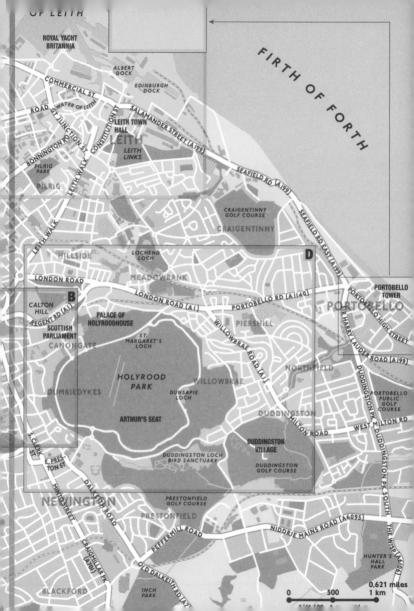

ELEPHANT HOUSE **ROYAL MILE WHISKY** **CHOCOLATE SOUP**

Tower (B A4)
→ *Museum of Scotland, Chambers St*
Tel. (0131) 225 3003
Daily noon–11pm
The Tower serves fine cuisine, using fresh Scottish ingredients to good effect. However, it is the outside terrace and fifth-floor view of the castle and the Edinburgh rooftops – especially at night – which makes this place so special. £20–30.

Vermilion (B A2)
→ *Scotsman Hotel, 20 North Bridge. Tel. (0131) 556 5565*
Wed–Sun 7–9.45pm
One of the hottest tables in Edinburgh since it opened in 2002, the restaurant of this designer hotel makes you feel a million dollars as you glide down its grand marble staircase to the dining room below. Feast on foie gras terrine with chocolate brioche and hazelnut ganache, followed by roast saddle of venison with a pear compote. £30.

CAFÉS

Chocolatesoup (B A3)
→ *2 Hunter Square*
Tel. (0131) 225 7669
Mon–Sat 8am–6pm (9am Sat); Sun 10am–6pm
Hmm, chocolate and soup – no, they don't come blended. Good choice of soups, sandwiches and yummy hot chocolates.

The Elephant House (B A4)
→ *21 George IV Bridge*
Tel. (0131) 220 5355
Daily 8am–10pm
Locations in Edinburgh where J. K. Rowling wrote the first *Harry Potter* are now as common as beds that Mary, Queen of Scots, slept in, and – as a sign proudly proclaims – the great Jo possibly did scribble bits here when not clutching a cuppa and a jumbo bun. The back room is where everyone wants to be, with views of the castle and Greyfriars. There is a sister Elephant at 37 Marshall St (**B** B5), between Potterrow and Nicolson Square. Oh, and the food is delicious and good value at both places.

Cafe Lucia (B B4)
→ *13-29 Nicolson St (Festival Theatre)*
Tel. (0131) 662 1112
Mon–Sat 10am–5.30pm; closed Sun, but open for performances
The Festival Theatre has the largest performing stage in Britain and is the home of Scottish Opera and Scottish Ballet; it is

also the heart of the Edinburgh Festival. There's a fine café selling delectable tarts – a good hang out when you're at a loose end or if it's pouring with rain outside.

Plaisir du Chocolat (Salon de The) (B C3)
→ *251-253 Canongate*
Tel. (0131) 556 9524
Mon–Sun 10am–6pm
Excellent French pastries, cakes and 75 tea varieties: the perfect expression of the Auld Alliance between France and Scotland. The shop also has fabulous chocolates to take away.

BARS

The Three Sisters (B A4)
→ *139 Cowgate*
Tel. (0131) 622 6801
Daily 9am–1am
One of many fine pubs (Bannerman's is another) along the Cowgate, this is regarded as one of the liveliest of Edinburgh's student pubs at night. During the day it makes a good pit stop.

SHOPPING

Stills Gallery (B A3)
→ *23 Cockburn St*
Tel. (0131) 622 6200 *Tue-Sat 10am–6pm (longer during Festival). www.stills.org*

One of Britain's premier photography galleries (established 1977), now also including some contemporary art. There are always exhibitions on and you can ponder buying a potential masterpiece over a cup of excellent coffee.

The Cigar Box (B B3)
→ *361 High St*
Tel. (0131) 225 3534
Mon-Sat 10am–6pm
www.thecigar.co.uk
If you like the smell of the best Cuban cigars, this is the place to visit: a traditional cigar emporium with all that the dedicated cigar smoker could want. Highly knowledgeable staff – they will give you all the advice you need.

Royal Mile Whiskies (B B3)
→ *379-381 High St*
Tel. (0131) 225 3383
Mon-Sat 10am–6pm; Sun 12.30–6pm
www.royalmilewhiskies.com
A huge selection of whiskies (over 300), bourbon and other liquors. Sample the various whiskies on offer, although it's unlikely you'll get to sample any of the 1930s vintages. As with Cigar Box (same management), the staff know their stuff and won't patronise you.

JOHN KNOX HOUSE MUSEUM

PARLIAMENT SQUARE
THE LOTHIAN HEART

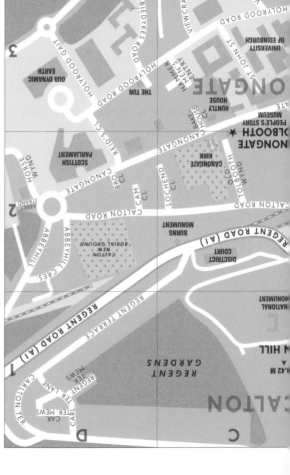

CANONGATE

OLD CALTON
N HILL

A.42 M

QUEEN'S DRIVE

DYKES ROAD

VIEWCRAIG ST

VIEWCRAIG ST

VIEWCR

NEW

VIEW

GARDENS

VIEWCRAIG

HOLYROOD ROAD

DUMBIEDYKES ROAD

HOLYROOD GAIT

HOLYROOD ROAD

ST JOHN'S

UNIVERSITY
OF EDINBURGH

OUR DYNAMIC
EARTH

THE TUN

HAMER.
ENTRY

BAKE.
HOUSE

HUNTLY
HOUSE
MUSEUM

PEOPLE'S STORY
MUSEUM

★ OLBOOTH

CANONGATE

CANONGATE
KIRK

REID'S CL.

CANONGATE

BRO.
CL.

LOCHEND
CL.

OLD
TOLBOOTH
WYND

CALTON ROAD

SCOTTISH
PARLIAMENT

HORSE
WYND

ABBEY
STRAND

CAM.
CL.

CALTON ROAD

BURNS
MONUMENT

REGENT ROAD (A1)

ABBEYHILL

ABBEYHILL CRES.

CALTON
NEW
BURIAL GROUND

DISTRICT
COURT

NATIONAL
MONUMENT

REGENT ROAD (A1)

REGENT TERRACE

REGENT
GARDENS

REGENT
TER
MEWS

CARLTON TER.

CAR
TER MEWS

CARLTON TER

3

2

1

D

C

CANONGATE TOLBOOTH

NELSON MONUMENT ON CALTON HILL

ersity's Talbot Rice Art ery houses a fine ction of Renaissance pean paintings.

ules Thorn Exhibition ental Museum (B B4)
Hill Square
131) 527 1649
Fri 2–4pm
t definitely not for the amish, this museum s the development of ery from 1505 to the ent day. 'Highlights' de a pocketbook made the skin of rsnatcher William Burke. r the Dental part...

y King's Close (B A3)
Warriston's Close
870 243 0160
Oct: daily 10am–9pm.

Nov–March: daily 10am–4pm (9pm Sat). Guided tours only www.realmarykingsclose.com
This subterranean warren of hidden streets beneath the City Chambers has recently been open to the public. It is weird, reputedly haunted and makes for a spooky trip back to 17th-century Edinburgh. A favorite site for paranormal investigation.

John Knox House Museum (B B3)
➔ *43-45 High St/Royal Mile*
Tel. (0131) 556 9579
July-Aug: Mon-Sat 10am–5pm (7pm Aug); Sun noon–4pm; Sep-June: Mon-Sat 10am–5pm
Aptly described as a medieval jewel, this is the house the greatest Scottish

Reformer John Knox (c.1513– 72) reputedly lived and died in. The house front, with its balconies and outside stairway, is remarkable.

Museum of Childhood (B B3)
➔ *42 High St*
Tel. (0131) 529 4412 Mon-Sat 10am–6pm (5pm Oct-May)
One for the family! Five floors packed with toys, games, books and displays relating to more serious issues such as children's health and education. Great fun for the wee ones – nostalgic for grown-ups!

Canongate Tolbooth (B C2)
➔ *163 Canongate*
Tel. (0131) 529 4057
Nestling beside the lovely

17th-century kirk, the Tolbooth (a former collection point for taxes dating from 1591) today contains reconstructions (sights, sounds and smells) of the lives of ordinary Edinburgh folk down the ages. A contrast to the more staid Huntly House directly opposite, which houses the Museum of Edinburgh.

Calton Hill (B C1)
➔ *East End of Princes St*
Probably the best place to view Edinburgh, with the City Observatory (1818), the imposing Nelson Monument and the National Monument, the latter being an 1820s attempt to copy the Pantheon – but the money ran out.

ROYAL BOTANIC GARDEN

SCOTTISH NATIONAL PORTRAIT GALLERY

Georgian House (C A5)

→ 7 Charlotte Square
Tel. (0131) 226 3318 March-
Oct: Mon-Sat 10am–5pm; Sun
2–5pm. www.nts.org.uk
One of the jewels in the
Robert Adam masterpiece
that is Charlotte Square:
Edinburgh's most exclusive
and maybe most attractive
square. Built in 1796, the
period rooms of the
Georgian House give a
fascinating insight into how
Edinburgh's 18th-century
wealthy class lived. The
house has recently been
lovingly restored by the
National Trust for Scotland,
and also contains
exceptional works by
Ramsay and Raeburn.

Royal Botanic Garden (C A2)

→ Inverleith Row
Tel. (0131) 552 7171 Daily
10am–7pm (6pm Oct-Feb)
www.rbge.org.uk
Established in 1670, the
conservation work of the
RBG is world-renowned:
take one of the twice-daily
tours if possible. Highlights
include the Rock Garden,
Alpine House, Heath
Garden, the arboretum and
the Chinese Hillside.

St Andrew's & St George's Church (C C5)

→ George Street
Tel. (0131) 225 3847
A superb building with an
innovative elliptical design
and much history (the
'Disruption' of the Church
of Scotland took place here
in 1843), St Andrew's
Church opened in 1784 and
merged congregations with
St George's of Charlotte
Square in the 1960s.
Conceived as essential
elements in the New Town
project, the churches were
designed to combine
spirituality with the
rationality of the Scottish
Enlightenment.

National Gallery of Scotland & Royal Scottish Academy (C C6)

→ The Mound, Princes Street
Tel. (0131) 624 6200
Daily 10am–5pm (7pm Thu)
www.nationalgalleries.org
Scotland's premier art
galleries were both
designed by William
Playfair to have maximum
impact as perfectly sited
masterpieces of
neoclassicism. The
National, opened in 185?
is particularly strong on
Scottish (Ramsay, Raeb
Wilkie, McTaggart…) and
Impressionist works, but
also houses sculptures
Bernini and masterpiec
by Raphael, Titian and
Rembrandt. Its predece
next door, today known
the Royal Scottish
Academy, was opened
1826 and has recently b
elegantly refurbished. I
features a wide-ranging
program of exhibitions.

C

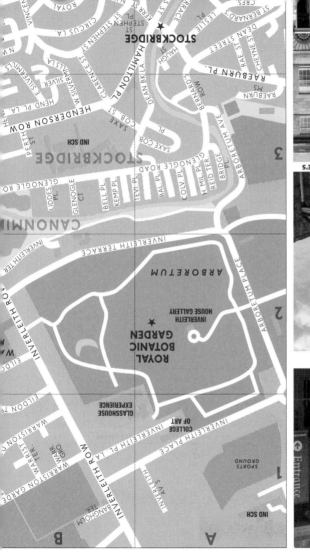

ROYAL BOTANIC GARDEN
ARBORETUM
INVERLEITH HOUSE GALLERY
GLASSHOUSE EXPERIENCE
STOCKBRIDGE
CANONMILLS

NATIONAL GALLERY OF SCOTLAND

ST ANDREW'S & ST GEORGE'S

Emerging from Waverley Station you come onto one of the noblest streets in the world. The impact of Princes Street is immediate: the grandeur of its flanking architecture, notably the Scott Monument and Balmoral hotel; the views of Calton Hill and Edinburgh Castle; and the magnificent Princes Street Gardens. Head north and walk the length of George Street to experience the vision behind the New Town project, and head further north for the resplendent Royal Botanic Garden and the stunning conservation area of Stockbridge, with its model housing and delightful walks – don't miss St Bernard's Well by the Leith.

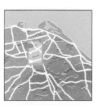

NO 28 CHARLOTTE SQUARE

THE ABBOTSFORD

RESTAURANTS

Henderson's (**C** C5)
→ 94 Hanover St
Tel. (0131) 225 2131
Daily noon–10pm (10.30pm Thu-Sat)
Using organic GM-free food and ethical in its attitude to suppliers, Henderson's has been an Edinburgh fixture for over 40 years. This self-service canteen-style eatery serves robust food and is a good place for celeb-spotting during the Festival (the table-service bistro is round the corner, at 25 Thistle St). The shop is glorious: stock up on delicacies to take home or just devour them on a bench outside. £12.

Café St Honoré (**C** C5)
→ 34 Thistle St NW Lane
Tel. (0131) 226 2211
Daily noon–2.15pm, 5.30–10pm (6pm Sat-Sun)
A classic French bistro down a cobbled lane, just the thing on a damp Edinburgh afternoon. Not cheap, but you'll feel good here and you will eat well (Le Café uses Scottish supplies to great French effect). £15–23.

No 28 Charlotte Square (**C** A5)
→ 28 Charlotte Square
(National Trust for Scotland)
Tel. (0131) 243 9339
Mon-Sat 9.30am–5pm (lunch served Mon-Fri noon–2.30pm); Sat noon–3.30pm
Food here is the full-portioned, old-fashioned Scotch style of dining. A lunch of broth, venison casserole, followed by a huge pudding is not for the fainthearted, but you will probably never eat in a more elegant dining room. Classy and understated in the best Edinburgh tradition. You should drop in for a coffee, at least. £16.

Opal Lounge (**C** C5)
→ 510 George St
Tel. (0131) 226 2275
Daily noon–10pm
Hugely popular and trendy, for many people this is the place to drink, see and be seen, while feasting on modern Asian-influenced cuisine. If you don't know what a bento box is you won't quite fit in, but you won't be made unwelcome either. Opal Lounge speaks of 'fusion-influenced street food', though the menu is a long way from any streets we know. Bento box £9.00 or £16.50 for two-courses.

CAFÉS

Queen Street Café (**C** D4)
→ Scottish National Portrait Gallery, 1 Queen St

JENNERS   **DICKSON & MACNAUGHTON**   **THE OXFORD BAR**

Tel. (0131) 557 2844
Mon-Sat 10am–4.30pm;
Sun 11am–4.30pm
A splendid café in a
splendid classical
building with Scotland's
most notable people on
the walls. You can ponder
the definition of 'notable'
with regard to some of the
moderns while eating
heartily and
inexpensively. The Scots
do scones well, and the
scones here, eaten with
raspberry jam and cream,
are out of this world.

Blue Moon Café (C D4)
➔ 36 Broughton St
Tel. (0131) 557 0911 Daily
11am–10pm (10am Sat-Sun)
A smart bar and a good
restaurant, but the café
element is the Cole Porter
tops. The Broughton St
area (the 'pink triangle') is
renowned for being gay-
friendly, but forget labels:
everyone's welcome here.

**Appetite@Rowlands
(C** B4)
➔ 42 Howe St
Tel. (0131) 225 3711
Mon-Fri 8.30am–4.30pm
Do not dismiss this neat
takeout place because of
the twee '@' or their offer
to do food in 'corporate
colors'; this lot cater to the
most demanding people
in Edinburgh and do well
at supplying fine gourmet

food to eat out or at home.
The eggplant caviar is
addictive. They also do
seriously good cocktails.

Circus Café (C B4)
➔ 15 N W Circus Place
Tel. (0131) 220 0333 Daily
10am–10.15pm (11pm bar)
Very popular with
Edinburgh's gilded youth.
Superb food (they bake
their own bread, buns and
lovely brioche), fresh
ingredients (fresh oysters
from Loch Fyne) and the
café is surprisingly child-
friendly for such a hip joint.

BARS

Café Royal (C D5)
➔ 17a & 19 West Register St
Tel. (0131) 556 1884
Mon-Sat 11am–11pm (1am
Fri-Sat); Sun 12.30–11pm
Come here for a clam
chowder and one of the
100 or so whiskies at the
huge oval bar (a haunt of
rugby fans). Reckoned by
some to have the best
pub food in Edinburgh,
the Café Royal Circle Bar
most certainly has great
seafood and fabulous
Victorian decor of carved
wood, green leather and
huge tiles dating from
1886. The Oyster Bar
(same quality food) at 17a
is also something of a
time machine to step into.

The Abbotsford (C C5)
➔ 3-5 Rose St (east end)
Tel. (0131) 225 5276
Mon-Sat 11am–11pm
Of all the bars in Rose St
we have to pick this one,
mainly because of the
fabulous building, but also
because, at the softy end
of the Rose St spectrum, it
makes a good start for a
pub crawl. And it serves
good food, unlike some.

The Oxford Bar (C B5)
➔ 8 Young St
Tel. (0131) 539 7119
Mon-Sat 11am–1am;
Sun 12.30pm–midnight
www.oxfordbar.com
A veritable institution once
described as 'the best old
man's pub in Edinburgh'
and, perhaps more
optimistically by its own
website as a 'scout hut for
the over 30s'. The Oxford,
a pub with long literary
traditions, has achieved
popular fame in our own
day by being the favored
haunt of both Inspector
Rebus and his creator, the
crime writer Ian Rankin.
Good beer and good
company.

SHOPPING

Jenners (C D5)
➔ 48 Princes St
Tel. (0131) 225 2442 Mon-
Wed, Fri-Sat 9am–5.30pm;

Thu 9am–7.30pm
www.jenners.com
One of Britain's oldest
department stores
(established in 1838) ,
selling all manner of luxury
goods, with particular
emphasis on classically
good Scottish products:
from knitwear to whisky.

Iain Mellis (C B4)
➔ 6 Baker's Place
Tel. (0131) 225 6566
Mon-Sat 9.30am–6pm
Cheesemonger Iain Mellis
came back to Scotland in
the mid-1990s to fill a huge
gap in the market for a
supplier of quality
farmhouse cheese, and his
enthusiastic, well-trained
staff will guide you through
what's on offer. Also sells a
wide range of fine deli
goods, from jams to hams.

**Dickson &
MacNaughton (C** C5)
➔ 21 Frederick St
Tel. (0131) 225 4218
Mon-Sat 9am–5.30pm
Worth a visit if only to get a
tweedy whiff of the real
'powers' that rule Britain.
The shop stocks most field-
related items (and a lot of
Burberry). The staff are
collectors' pieces in
themselves: discreet and
with that coiled, elegant
Edinburgh deference that
lives just on the polite side
of condescension.

STOCKBRIDGE

SCOTT MONUMENT

Map labels:

BONNINGTON

ST MARKS PARK

WARRISTON

WARRISTON CEMETERY

BROUGHTON

WATER OF LEITH

WARRISTON ROAD

BROUGHTON ROAD

POWDERHALL ROAD

BEAVERHALL ROAD

DUNEDIN STREET

LOGIE MILL

LOGIE GDNS

GREEN ROAD

BEAVERBANK PL

BOAT GDN

WARRISTON ROAD

CANON MILLS

HUNT ST

BELLEVUE ROAD

BELLEVUE GARDENS

W ANN ST

ANN ST

BELLEVUE ST

BELL ST

BELLEVUE PLACE

LA MELGUND

MELGUND TER

BELLEVUE TER

EAST CLAREMONT STREET

CLAREMONT CRES

CLAREMONT GRO

BK

CLAREMONT ST

BELLEVUE CRESCENT

COR

BELLEVUE

BELLEVUE SEC SCH

MANSFIELD PL

RODNEY ST

HERIOT HILL TER

BROUGHTON ST

EYRE PLACE

EYRE TER

EYRE CRES

CANON LA

LON LA

KING GEORGE V PARK

SCOTLAND ST

W SCOTLAND ST

ST LA

ROYAL CRESCENT

DUNDAS ST

N E LANE

ROW

LONDON ST

DRUMMOND PLACE

NELSON ST

DONALD ST

S E LANE

NEW BRO

BARONY ST

BROUGHTON ST

BROUGHTON PLACE

BROUGHTON ST LA

DUBLIN ST

N E LANE

MEUSE

ALBANY ST LA

ALBANY ST

MKT

STREET

D STREET

C

D

1

2

3

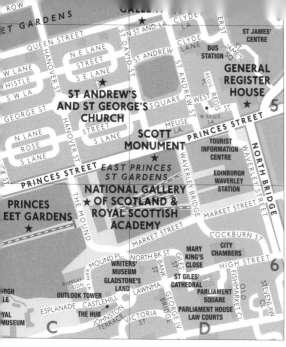

GENERAL REGISTER HOUSE

ST BERNARD'S WELL BY STOCKBRIDGE

**tish National
rait Gallery (C D4)**
ueen Street
131) 624 7126
as above
ed in a lovely red
stone building
eled on the Doges'
e in Venice), dating
the 1880s, the NPG's
ction includes portraits
st notable Scots,
and bad, from Mary,
n of Scots, to Sean
ery. Also here is the
nal photograph
ction, including works
vid Octavius Hill and
rt Adamson.

kbridge (C A4)
ally a self-contained
attractive) village, the

old Stockbridge was neatly
absorbed into the Georgian
New Town in the 18th
century. Look out also for
the Stockbridge 'colonies'
by the river: workers'
dwellings built by the
Edinburgh Building Co-
operative 1861–1911, and
the ancient St Bernard's
Well with its 1789 'Roman'
temple.

Scott Monument (C D5)
→ *East Princes St Gardens*
Tel. (0131) 529 4068
Mon-Sat 9am–6pm; Sun
10am–6pm (3pm Oct-March)
Designed and built by a
local craftsman, this
monument to Sir Walter
Scott (the world's largest for
a writer) was completed in

1846. It stands 200 ft high
(you can climb to the top
gallery and admire the view)
and contains at the base a
twice life-size statue of
Scott in Carrera marble.

**Princes St
Gardens (C C6)**
→ *Open daily dawn 'till dusk*
These stunning gardens
were the site of the artificial
Nor'Loch in 1490, before
subsequently being used
as a dumping ground by the
Old Towners in the centuries
that followed. Eventually
protected from develop-
ment by Parliament in 1816,
the gardens remain some
of the finest municipal
gardens anywhere; the
floral clock (built 1903) is

the oldest floral clock
in the world.

**General Register
House (C D5)**
→ *2 Princes Street*
Tel. (0131) 535 1314 Mon-Fri:
9am–4.45pm (disabled
access) www.nas.gov.uk
Designed by Robert Adam
and completed in 1789 to
house Scotland's public
records (of which the
earliest surviving one dates
from the 12th century), this
gorgeous building opposite
the grand Balmoral Hotel
dominates the east end of
Princes St. An annex to this
building, West Register
House, built in 1814 to
another design by Adam,
stands in Charlotte Square.

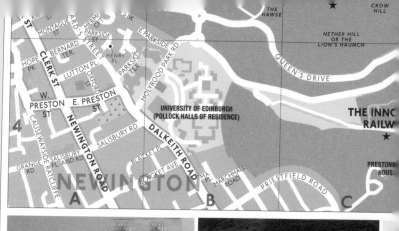

SCOTTISH PARLIAMENT

OUR DYNAMIC EARTH

DU

The Innocent Railway (**D** C4)

Once a busy railway line, dubbed 'The Innocent Railway' either because no one ever died on it or because it was very slow! Now a cycle and jogging path, it is a perfect way to spend a sunny afternoon.

Palace of Holyroodhouse

→ Tel. (0131) 556 7371
Daily 9.30am–6pm (4.30pm Nov-March). Closed during Royal visits. Last entry 60 mins before closing time
www.royal.gov.uk

The Queen's official residence when in Scotland, Holyroodhouse started as an annex to the abbey above before being expanded into a palace for James IV in 1498. Mary, Queen of Scots, lived here 1561–67 and was married twice in the abbey. The Palace is the setting for Walter Scott's *Waverley*. Little remains of the original buildings – the current Baroque masterpiece was mostly built under Charles II in the 1670s.

Holyrood Abbey (**D** B2)

→ *Holyrood Park (access via the Palace of Holyroodhouse)*
Tel. (0131) 668 8800

Now a highly romantic ruin, this Augustinian abbey was founded in 1128 by King David I, the name deriving from an alleged piece of the True Cross, or 'rood' in ancient Scots, donated by David's mother, St Margaret.

The Queen's Gallery (**D** B2)

→ *Palace of Holyroodhouse*
Tel. (0131) 556 5100
Hours as above

Built in the shells of a former church and school, the gallery opened in 2002 to display a selection from the Queen's collection (one of the richest private art collections in the world). This is the first permanent exhibition space in Scotland for these artworks.

Arthur's Seat (**D** C3)

→ *Holyrood Park*

Situated in Holyrood P (650 acres), Arthur's Se an extinct volcano, has highest (822 ft) vantage point in the city. The 20 30-minute walk to the worth the effort, as the views of the city below spectacular. The park i is protected as a Sched Ancient Monument, wi medieval ruined chape grandeur of Salisbury C and much wildlife.

Scottish Parliament (

→ *Holyrood*
Tel. (0131) 348 5200
All year: Tue-Thu 9am-7p Sat-Sun 10am-4pm. April-Oct: Mon and Fri 10 6pm; Nov-March 10am-4

D

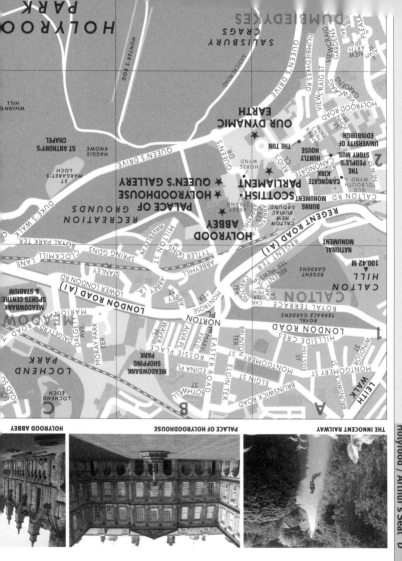

THE INNOCENT RAILWAY

PALACE OF HOLYROODHOUSE

HOLYROOD ABBEY

HOLYROO PARK

DUMBIEDYKES

SALISBURY CRAGS

QUEEN'S DRIVE

RADICAL ROAD

HUNTER'S BOG

DUMBIEDYKES RD

VIEW·CRAIG ST

VIEW·CRAIG GARDENS

ADAM ST

PLEASA

NEW

NEW

WHINNY HILL

HOLYROOD ROAD

SAINT JOHN ST

VIEW·CRAIG GDNS

HILL

OUR DYNAMIC EARTH

THE TUN

UNIVERSITY OF EDINBURGH

CHAPEL

ST ANTHONY'S

HAGGIS KNOWE

QUEEN'S DRIVE

ST MARGARET'S LOCH

DUKE'S WALK

QUEEN'S

DR.

HORSE WYND

REID'S

CANONGATE

HUNTLY HOUSE

STORY MUS

THE PEOPLE'S STORY MUS

THE PEOPLE'S KIRK CANONGATE

OLD TOLBOOTH WYND

RECREATION

★ **QUEEN'S GALLERY** ★

★ **HOLYROODHOUSE** ★

PALACE OF GROUNDS

SCOTTISH · PARLIAMENT

MONUMENT

CALTON RD

NEW BURIAL GROUND

CALTON

ABBEY STRAND

★ ABBEY WYND ★

BURNS MONUMENT

HOLYROOD ABBEY

WAVERLEY

MILTON

TYLER GDNS

SPRING GDNS

ABBEYHILL

STANLEY

ABBEY ST

ABBEY LA.

MILTON

MONTROSE TER

CARLTON TER

TER MEWS

REGENT TER

REGENT GARDENS

TER MEWS

CAR

CAR TER MEWS

REGENT ROAD [A1]

NATIONAL MONUMENT

HILL 100.42 M

CALTON

ROYAL TERRACE

ROYAL TERRACE GARDENS

BRUNTON TER

LONDON ROAD

HILLSIDE CRES

HILLSIDE ST

MONTGOMERY ST

ROYAL PARK TER

CLOCKMILL LANE

LOWER LONDON RD

LONDON ROAD [A1]

MARIONVILLE RD

DALGETY AVE

DALGETY RD

MORAY PARK TER

MARIONFIELD PL

MARIONFIELD

EASTER ROAD

ALVA PLACE

NORTON PL.

ROSSIE PLACE

EASTER EDINA PL

MEADOWBANK SHOPPING PARK

MEADOWBANK SPORTS CENTRE & STADIUM

MEADOWBANK

LOCHEND PARK

LOCHEND LOCH

LOCHEND ROAD

BOTHWELL ST

BRUNSWICK ROAD

ELGIN ST

ELGIN TER

BRUNSWICK ST

WINDSOR ST

MONTGOMERY ST

HILLSIDE

BRUNSWICK ST

LEITH WALK

LEITH

A

B

1

2

medieval king, really rest on the hill's rocky seat? The hill emerged 300 million years ago after the earth opened during a volcanic eruption. Incongruously and rather dramatically standing in the center of the city, it dominates the Abbey and Palace of Holyroodhouse – both witnesses to major events in Scotland's history: the new Scottish Parliament and the striking roof of Our Dynamic Earth. Take a break from the city center and explore Duddingston Village; experience the peace of the Loch, a sanctuary for migrating birds, and visit the ancient Kirk, its lovely 'secret' garden and its small tower, where the rules of curling were devised.

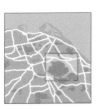

SHEEP HEID INN

VALVONA & CROLLA

RESTAURANTS

Pizza Express (**D** A2)
→ 111 Holyrood Rd
Tel. (0131) 332 7229 Daily 11am–10pm (11pm Fri-Sat)
The fierce competition in Edinburgh amongst restaurants means even basic pit stops like Pizza Express have to raise their game, and the Holyrood one is exemplary. It also helps that the staff are pleasant. Modern Italian food. Pizza £7–10.

Fenwicks (**D** A4)
→ 15 Salisbury Place
Tel. (0131) 667 4265
Daily noon–2pm, 6pm–late
Mainly patronized by cash-strapped students, Fenwicks serves honest, hearty, affordable, contemporary Scottish cuisine with a continental influence. Peaceful, cozy ambience. The staff are especially proud of the fact that Inspector Rebus brunches here in *The Falls*. No-smoking. £18.

Calistoga (**D** A4)
→ 93 St Leonard's St
Tel. (0131) 668 4207
Thu-Mon 6–11pm (10pm Sun) and lunch Fri, Mon 12.30–2.30pm
Edinburgh's first Californian restaurant, serving only Californian wine. Miso soup with tofu,

citrus-steamed seabass with lemon zesty rice and mango ginger coulis are amongst the dishes on offer. The three-course lunch for £14 is a bargain. No-smoking restaurant, obviously.

Erawan Oriental (**D** A2)
→ Unit 4, The Tun
Tel. (0131) 556 4242
Mon-Sat noon–2.30pm, 5.30–10pm; Sun 6–9.30pm
Edinburgh is strong on Thai restaurants and Erawan is as good as you'll find in any city, with an extensive separate menu for vegetarians. It's a very smart restaurant, but its proximity to the Scottish Parliament means you may have to endure the bagpipe drone of a charmless Minister of Scottish Parliament at the next table. £23.

CAFÉS

Beanscene (**D** A2)
→ 67 Holyrood Road
Tel. (0131) 557 6549
Mon-Sat 7.30am–8.30pm (11pm summer); Sun 9am–8.30pm (11pm summer)
www.beanscene.co.uk
All ten Scottish outlets are eerily like the mothership in Glasgow both in decor and staff, but that's no reason to complain when

Y SANCTUARY

BAGPIPE GALORE

THE ENGINE SHED

service is as good as this. Amazingly they manage to combine tasty, reasonably priced food and child-friendliness with being hip music venues at night – an uncommon act to pull off.

The Engine Shed Café (D A3)

➔ 19 St Leonard's Lane
Tel. (0131) 662 0040
Mon-Thu 10.30am–3.30pm, Fri 10.30am–2.30pm
www.engineshed.org.uk
Inspired by Rudolf Steiner's teaching, this vegetarian/vegan café provides employment for adults with learning difficulties. In a lovely reversal of the usual Rebus endorsement, they are proud of the fact that Rankin's gloomy Inspector does not eat here:
'Though a one-minute walk from his office, Inspector Rebus had never eaten at The Engine Shed. Everything about it was too healthy, too nutritious...' (Dead Souls).

Metropole (D A4)

➔ 33 Newington Road
Tel. (0131) 668 4999
Daily 9am–1pm
Affordable (delicious salads and large cakes) and yet with a stylish feel; child-friendly too. This is all that you could want.

WINE BAR, BARS

Valvona & Crolla (D A1)

➔ 19 Elm Row (Leith Walk)
Tel. (0131) 556 6066
Mon-Sat 8am–late;
Sun 11am–5.30pm
www.valvonacrolla.co.uk
At the back of one of the city's best delis in Scotland is one of the best-value places to feast on Italian home cooking. Great family place, great service and great prices: this wine bar/café is as good as eating out gets. It now has an equally impressive sister outlet, VinCaffè, at 11 Multrees Walk (in Clyde Lane), Tel. 557 0088 (C D5).

The Tun Bar and Kitchen (D A2)

➔ Holyrood Road
Tel. (0131) 557 9297
Daily 11am–11pm (7pm Sun)
People mainly come here to linger over a drink and check out this expensive development. The Tun is central to the hoped-for establishment of a 'campus Holyrood', and is haunted by scarily well-off young professionals.

Jenny Ha's (D A2)

➔ 65 Canongate
Tel. (0131) 556 2101
Mon-Sat 11am–11pm;
Sun 12.30–11pm
'Ha' means 'lucky'; hence

the success of this busy, large boozer. The original 17th-century tavern, just to the east of the current hostelry, was demolished by philistines in 1960.

The Regent (D B1)

➔ 2 Montrose Terrace
Tel. (0131) 661 8198
Mon-Sat 11am–1am;
Sun 12.30pm–1am
A recently established and very popular gay bar – ales are good and the atmosphere is friendly, as it also is in the Stag & Turret just along the road (1–7 Montrose Terrace).

Sheep Heid Inn (D D3)

➔ 43 The Causeway
Tel. (0131) 656 6951 Mon-Sat 11am–11pm (midnight Thu-Sat); Sun 12.30–11pm
The Sheep Heid Inn dates from 1360 (with some rebuilding, one assumes) and claims to be the country's oldest pub. Pleasingly sited in the beautiful Duddingston village, it's a favorite end to a walk down from Arthur's Seat. Good-value food and a charming beer garden with a skittle alley.

SHOPPING

Abbey Sanctuary (D A2)

➔ Abbey Sanctuary
Abbey Strand, Canongate
Tel. (0131) 557 2365

Daily 9.30am–6pm (5pm Nov-March)
Built around 1500, partially rebuilt in 1544 and fully restored in 1916, this impressive building houses the Historic Scotland bookshop and Information Center. The friendly staff will answer any questions you may have about Edinburgh's past.

Bagpipes Galore (D A2)

➔ 82 Canongate
Tel. (0131) 556 4073
Mon-Sat 9.30am–5.15pm
www.bagpipe.co.uk
Housed in an absolute gem of a building, this shop claims to make and sell more bagpipes than any other company in the UK. Its atmosphere is refreshingly non-tacky given the lava of tat flowing down the Royal Mile, and you can buy any bagpipe accessory here.

The Old Children's Bookshelf (D A2)

➔ 175 Canongate
Tel. (0131) 558 3411 Mon-Sat 10.30am–5pm (times vary)
Yes, you can shop on Amazon, but it will never be as good as browsing in here – a friendly, hassle-free children's bookstore selling all kinds of books, from annuals to prints. A treasure.

THE QUEEN'S GALLERY

ARTHUR'S SEAT

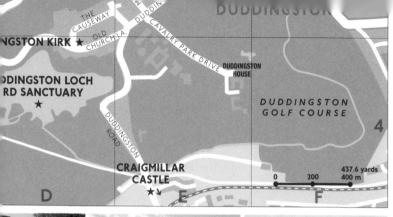

THE CAUSEWAY · OLD CHURCH LA · *DUDDIN* · CAVALRY PARK DRIVE

GSTON KIRK ★

DUDDINGSTON HOUSE

DDINGSTON LOCH
RD SANCTUARY
★

DUDDINGSTON ROAD

DUDDINGSTON GOLF COURSE

4

CRAIGMILLAR CASTLE
★↘

437.6 yards
0   200   400 m

D   E   F

DUDDINGSTON LOCH BIRD SANCTUARY

CRAIGMILLAR CASTLE

scottish.parliament.uk
building's designer, late
an architect Enric
les, drew his inspiration
'the surrounding land-
e, the flower paintings
arles Rennie Mac-
sh and the upturned
s on the seashore'. The
Parliament, built by
les' practice and a
ish company in a
are of steel, oak and
e, opened in 2004. As
ll innovative buildings,
egarded as either a
erpiece or a huge waste
oney; either way, it is
a visit.
Dynamic Earth (**D** A2)
lyrood Road

*Tel. (0131) 550 7800 Daily
10am–5pm (6pm July-Aug).
Last entry 70 mins before
closing time.
www.dynamicearth.co.uk*
One of Edinburgh's main
attractions since opening in
1999, the center is a family-
orientated journey through
the processes that have
shaped our Earth. The latest
technology (virtual rides,
simulations, etc.) makes it a
fantastically real experience
(allow at least two hours).
Duddingston Kirk (**D** D4)
➔ *Tel. (0131) 661 4240
www.duddingston-kirk.org.uk*
Situated in the conservation
area of Duddingston Village
(where Bonnie Prince Charlie

stayed), this lovely Norman
church is one of the oldest
churches in continual use in
Scotland. Many famous
names are linked with the
kirk: Walter Scott was an
elder here and the 'Pinkerton
Window' commemorates the
wife of the great detective
Alan Pinkerton.
**Duddingston Loch
Bird Sanctuary** (**D** D4)
➔ *Holyrood Park*
A pretty little natural loch,
this is an ideal spot for
birdwatchers or just for a
quiet picnic: the loch itself
forms the setting for one of
Scotland's most iconic
paintings, *Portrait of the
Reverend Robert Walker*

Skating, attributed to
Raeburn.
Craigmillar Castle
(off map, south of E4)
➔ *Craigmillar
Tel. (0131) 661 4445 March-
Sep: Sat-Wed 9.30am–4pm
www.historic-scotland.gov.uk*
Just south of Holyrood Park,
this massive 14th- to 15th-
century town house, with its
towers and enclosure,
speaks of troubled times.
Mary, Queen of Scots, stayed
here after the murder of her
secretary, David Rizzio, at
Holyroodhouse, while her
advisors counseled killing
her husband, Darnley, the
major suspect of Rizzio's
death.

DEAN VILLAGE

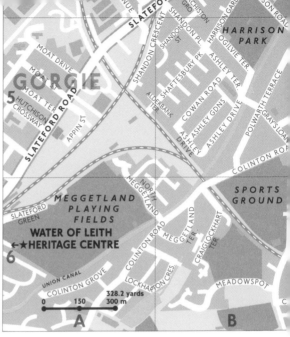

A

B

EDINBURGH ZOO

Scottish National Gallery of Modern Art (**E** B2)
➔ 75 Belford Road
Tel. (0131) 624 6200
Daily 10am–5pm
www.nationalgalleries.org
Housed in a bright and airy neoclassical 1820s building, the gallery's large collection is particularly strong on early 20th-century French and Russian art; British and particularly Scottish art is also well represented.

St Mary's Episcopal Cathedral (**E** C2)
➔ Palmerston Place
Tel. (0131) 225 6293
Daily 7.15am–6pm (9pm summer). Disabled access through the West Door
www.cathedral.net
A magnificent 19th-century episcopal church, St Mary's was designed by Sir George Gilbert Scott in his trademark Gothic style and was opened in 1879. The new stained-glass windows were designed by Eduardo Paolozzi. St Mary's choir is one of the finest in the UK.

Leamington Lift Bridge (**E** D3)
➔ www.edinburgh architecture.co.uk
Built in 1896 and originally located on Fountainbridge, this impressive piece of engineering has been newly restored as part of the link between the Union Canal in Edinburgh and the Forth and Clyde Canal, thus joining Glasgow and Edinburgh again by canal. The bridge is open to pedestrians and cyclists.

Edinburgh Zoo (off map, west of A2)
➔ Corstorphine Road
Tel. (0131) 334 9171 April-Sep: daily 9am–6pm; Oct-March: daily 9am–5pm (4.30pm)
www.edinburghzoo.org.uk
Zoos may have a bad press these days, but Edinburgh's zoo (founded 1913) has an excellent record in conservation and education. With 600,000 visitors a year, this is one of Scotland's big attractions.

Murrayfield Rugby Stadium (**E** A3)
➔ Tel. (0131) 346 5000
Tours by appt: Mon-Fri 11am–2.30pm; Sat-Sun b arrangement. www.sru.o
Opened in 1925, this is of the world's greatest rugby grounds, frequen selling out to its 67,500 capacity. There is alway truly passionate (but n threatening) atmosphe especially when the 'A Enemy' is playing.

Water of Leith Visito Centre (off map, west
➔ 24 Lanark Road
Tel. (0131) 455 7367

E

ST MARY'S EPISCOPAL CATHEDRAL

SCOTTISH NATIONAL GALLERY OF MODERN ART

...spend a week exploring west Edinburgh's stunning architecture and many fine attractions, from the exquisite Dean Village in the north to the Water of Leith Walkway winding south. Visit Murrayfield when Scotland play and hear the Bravehearts sing as they get beaten (again!); take the children to the zoo or to Gorgie City Farm; spend some quiet time in the Dean and Modern Art galleries; or shop to your heart's content – the shops around William and Stafford streets are particularly elegant and uplifting, and mercifully tat-free.

CAFÉ NEWTON

WILLIAM STREET

RESTAURANTS

Howies One
Alva St (E D2)
→ 1a Alva St
Tel. (0131) 225 5553 Daily
noon–3pm, 5.30–10pm
www.howies.uk.com
There are now four Alvas in Edinburgh and the group (they dislike the term 'chain') is growing: popular with locals and very good value for money, this is fine Scottish and European cooking with a care for tradition and good innovation. Set lunch £8.50; dinner £15.95.

Songkran (E D2)
→ 24A Stafford St
Tel. (0131) 225 7889
Mon–Sat noon–2.30pm,
5.30–11pm
This highly regarded Thai restaurant (with a sister branch in Stockbridge) has an elaborate and quite extensive range of Thai cuisine. The decor is standard Thai restaurant kitsch, but is not too oppressive. Set lunch £9 and set dinner £20.

Bar Roma (E D1)
→ 39a Queensferry St
Tel. (0131) 226 2977
Sun–Thu noon–midnight;
Fri–Sat noon–1am
www.bar-roma.co.uk
Hugely popular trattoria with lots of choice: does the classic pizza and pasta dishes well.
£18–£26.

Cuba Norte (E D2)
→ 192 Morrison St
Tel. (0131) 221 1430
Daily noon–11pm (6–11pm
Sun in winter)
Pretty fair Latin food of the type that's not too difficult to get right, such as fajitas and enchiladas, but there's a great party spirit about the place. A favorite destination for the younger crowd. £20.

The Restaurant (E A2)
→ 29 Roseburn Terrace
Tel. (0131) 476 7209 Tue–Sat
noon–2pm, 6–10pm;
Sun 11am–2pm, 6–9pm
Has a great reputation for using classic, fresh local ingredients in a modern way. Some may feel that caramelising turnips is stretching traditional Scottish food a bit, but this is a seriously good place to eat out. Foodies will love it, and it's not expensive for what it is. Set lunch £7.50 or £9.50 excl. wine; dinner £21.

Channings Bar and Restaurant (E C1)
→ Channings Hotel, 15
South Leamonth Gardens
Tel. (0131) 315 2225
Mon–Fri noon–3pm;
Sat–Sun 12.30–3.30pm; daily

HELEN BATEMAN

GALLERY CAFÉ

STUDIO ONE

6–10pm (11pm Fri-Sat)
Since merging with the Ochre Vita brasserie here, Channings is now set in the conservatory of this stylish hotel. Still retaining its impeccable yet relaxed service, its menu has become more flexible and affordable. The wine list is good value, with minimal mark-up on the more expensive wines. £22.

CAFÉS

Gallery Café (E B1)
→ 74 Belford Road (Scottish National Gallery of Modern Art)
Tel. (0131) 332 8600
Daily 10am–4.30pm
A very fine museum café with a great alfresco option. When the weather's favorable, you can sit out in the garden among the sculptures. Great choice of healthy, inexpensive food.

Café Provençal (E D2)
→ 34 Alva St
Tel. (0131) 220 6105
Mon-Wed 8am–8pm; Thu-Fri 8am–10.30pm
A fine French café aimed at lunching professionals and ladies meeting pals for a 'blether'; they import a lot of their ingredients and obviously care about the food.

Café Newton (E B1)
→ The Dean Gallery, 72 Belford Rd
Tel. (0131) 624 6273
Mon-Sun 10am–4.30pm
www.nationalgalleries.org
A table-service café with a relaxed ambience and arty black and white photographs on the wall. You will have to queue at lunchtime, but the food – especially the cakes – is well worth the short wait.

BARS

The Diggers (Athletic Arms) (E B4)
→ 1-3 Angle Park Terrace
Tel. (0131) 337 3822
Mon-Sat open till midnight; closes 6pm Sunday
Nicknamed 'The Diggers' because it is by a graveyard, this is a friendly traditional pub (food is basically pie 'n' chips) with good beer and good staff; the 80-shilling beer is recommended. It is located near Tynecastle and Murrayfield, so is a launching pub for Hearts fans and rugby crowds before home matches.

Caley Sample Room (E B4)
→ 58 Angle Park Terrace
Tel. (0131) 337 7204
Mon-Thu & Sun open until midnight; Fri-Sat, until 1am

Like The Diggers, a traditional pub with a strong Hearts-supporting client base. It uses barrels for tables and has good cask-conditioned ales.

Rutland No 1 (E D2)
→ 3 Rutland St
Tel. (0131) 229 3402
Daily 10am–1am
Imposing corner pub with a rather intimidating serious-drinker bar inside. The spiral staircase is best not examined too closely after a few pints of the fine beer. Busy, lively and very friendly.

Harry's Bar (E D1)
→ 78 Randolph Place
Tel. (0131) 539 8100
Daily noon–1pm
Though billed rather optimistically as Edinburgh's 'New York' bar, this is a good attempt at an NY-kinda place for homesick Americans. The conservatory view out back is surprisingly nice.

SHOPPING

William Street/ Stafford Street
To the west of Princes St you will find one of the classiest shopping areas in any city: three representative shops are listed here, but there are other many fine boutiques

and designer shops in the area, from Sam Thomas (18 Stafford St) to Extra Inch Ltd (12 William St). This is one of the chicest parts of Edinburgh.

Helen Bateman (E D2)
→ 16 William Street
Tel. (0131) 220 4495
Mon-Sat 9.30am–6pm
www.helenbateman.com
This is one for the girls. Fine shoes and boots designed by Helen; deservedly very popular and now expanding to other cities (check out the excellent website for mail-order details).

Studio One Gallery (E D2)
→ 10 Stafford Street
Tel. (0131) 226 5812 Mon-Fri 9.30am–6pm (Thu 7pm, Sat 5.30pm); Sun noon–5pm
Good one-stop shop to buy a range of classy souvenirs. The gallery exhibits and sells ceramics, glass, wooden objects and jewelry.

Arkangel (E D2)
→ 4 William Street
Tel. (0131) 226 4466
Mon-Sat 10am–5.30pm
(Thu 6.30pm)
Not cheap but upmarket even for Edinburgh; stocks the ultra-hip Scottish designer Hillary Rohde's cashmere clothes.

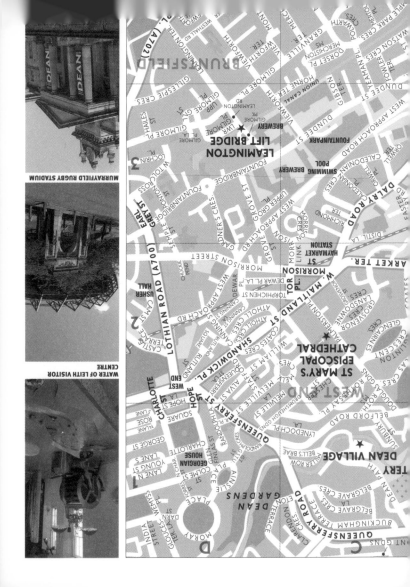

MURRAYFIELD RUGBY STADIUM

WATER OF LEITH VISITOR CENTRE

BRUNSFIELD

LEAMINGTON LIFT BRIDGE

BREWERY

FOUNTAINPARK

SWIMMING POOL

BREWERY

DALRY ROAD

HAYMARKET STATION

W. MAITLAND ST

USHER HALL

ST MARY'S EPISCOPAL CATHEDRAL

WEST END

WEST END

GEORGIAN HOUSE

DEAN VILLAGE

DEAN GARDENS

QUEENSFERRY ROAD

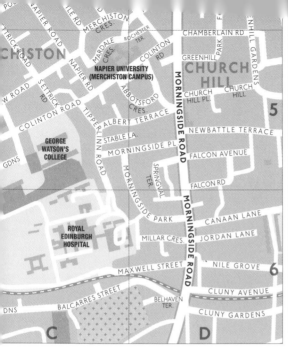

DEAN CEMETERY

GORGIE CITY FARM

10am–4pm (closed
Tue in Oct–March).
d Dec 24–early Jan
waterofleith.org.uk
erb child-friendly
tion with lots of scope
mily involvement, it is
eal introduction to the
hidden natural and
fe heritage. The Leith
way is 12 miles long,
ell worth setting aside
for.

Village (E C1)
w.deanvillage.org
ranquil area, originally
illage of the Water of
('dean' means 'deep
'), is only a ten-minute
from the west of
es St and was a water-

milling community as far
back as the 12th century.
Worth a look are Dean
Bridge, built in 1831 by
Telford; the 18th-century
Bell's Brae Bridge; Well
Court (1884, housing for the
mill's workers); and Dean
Cemetery (see below).

Dean Cemetery (E C1)
→ *Dean Path*
www.headstones.fsnet.co.uk
This well maintained and
historically important
graveyard opened in 1846
and has some fascinating
monuments. Notable
headstones include those
for photography pioneer
Octavius Hill, Lord Cockburn
and General Sir Hector

Macdonald. A humble
private whose heroics in
Afghanistan began his rise,
Sir Hector (subject of the
lovely waltz tune 'Hector the
Hero', killed himself in 1903
after he was accused of
being homosexual. The
story that his grave is empty,
that death was faked and
that he assumed the identi-
ty of the German Colonel von
Mackensen *is* just a story.

Dean Gallery (E B1)
→ *73 Belford Rd*
Tel. (0131) 624 6200
Daily 10am–5pm
www.nationalgalleries.org
Opened in 1999 to house
Edinburgh-born Eduardo
Paolozzi's gift of sculpture

and graphic art, the gallery
is also home to the very
impressive Dada and
Surrealist collection of the
Gallery of Modern Art. The
building itself dates from
the 1830s and was origi-
nally an orphan's hospital.

Gorgie City Farm (E B4)
→ *51 Gorgie Road*
Tel. (0131) 337 4202
Daily 9.30am–4.30pm
(closes 4pm in winter months)
Established in 1982 to bring
something of country life to
the city, the farm won a
'child-friendly' award in
1995, and is a model of its
kind. It's great for the kids
and also a good place to
shop for organic produce.

BONNINGTON IND EST

LEITH

BONNINGTO

BONNINGTON

BONNINGTON RD

PILRIG PARK

SPRINGFIELD

BONNIGHAUGH

STEWARTFIELD

NEWHAVEN RD

REDBRAES PL/D

BROUGHTON ROAD

WATER OF LEITH

BONNINGTON
ST MARK'S PARK

ROSEBANK CEMETERY

PILRIG STREET

PILRIG GDNS

PILRIG

BALFOUR PL

CAMBRIDGE GDNS

CAMBRIDGE STREET

CAMBRIDGE AVE

SPRINGFIELD ST

STEAD'S

LEITH WA

LEITH

POWDERHALL RD

LOGIE MILL
BEAVERHALL RD
LOGIE MILL

MCDONALD ROAD

ROSSLYN CRES

LO

4

A   B   C

TRINITY HOUSE

PORTOBELLO BEACH

LEITH CUSTOM

Lamb's House (F D3)
→ Burgess Street
www.undiscoveredscotland.
co.uk/edinburgh
Disregard claims that Mary,
Queen of Scots, slept here
on her return from France;
this fine house was built
some time after her death
in the early 1600s for a
prosperous merchant called
Andrew Lamb. It is now a
day centre for old people.

Leith Links (F E3-4)
→ www.scottishgolfhistory.net
This unassuming stretch of
municipal grass is a place of
pilgrimage for golfers. As far
back as the 1590s, kirk
elders were complaining
that men would rather play

golf on the Links than go to
church, and the first golf
international took place
here in 1681 between
England (two noblemen)
and Scotland (the Duke of
York and a local cobbler).
The first formal rules for golf
were drawn up here in the
1740s.

Royal Yacht Britannia (F C1)
→ Ocean Terminal
Tel. (0131) 555 5566
March-Oct: 9.30am–6pm.
Nov-Feb: 10am–5pm. Last
admission 90 mins before
closing time; fully accessible
to wheelchair users.
www.royalyachtbritannia.co.uk
Allow at least 90 mins for

your visit to one of the
world's most famous ships.
Built in 1953, Britannia
carried the Queen on 968
official voyages. The Royal
Apartments are full of
evocative mementos; a
particular favorite of many
is the Baby Grand, played
by Princess Diana whenever
she stayed on the ship.

St Margaret's Church
(F map, south of F4)
→ Restalrig Road South
Tel. (0131) 554 7400
www.st-margarets-church.com
A 6th-century saint,
Triduana, is said to be
buried here – note the
unusual hexagonal 15th-
century well and chapel.

Legends apart, the orig
of this intriguing churc
with templar connecti
go back to at least the
century. Destroyed dur
the Reformation it was
rebuilt in 1837 by Willia
Burn in the Scotch bar
style. It has fine staine
glass, old monuments
ancient tomsbtones.

Leith Police Station
→ Queen Charlotte Stree
Tel. (0131) 554 9350
www.theleither.net
Formerly Leith Town Ha
and built in 1824 to be
court house and event
the Town Hall of the
burgeoning port of Leit
you're here in Leith Fes

F

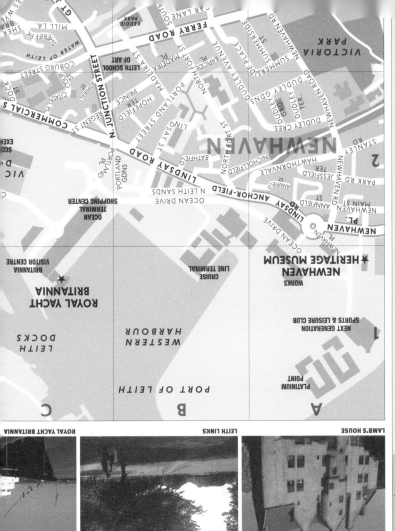

ROYAL YACHT BRITANNIA · LEITH LINKS · LAMB'S HOUSE

Scotland's principal and busiest commercial port. Its old Georgian and Victorian warehouses built to hold wine (especially claret), whisky or dry goods have now been converted into offices and upmarket apartments. Although (as it is always said) much has changed in Leith since the movie *Trainspotting* was made, the dark side spurned by Ewan MacGregor's Renton is still there. Here Edinburgh is, as ever, the city of Jekyll and Hyde – from the new wine bars and classy restaurants of the Shore to the pubs of Great Junction Street is no great journey, but a journey adjoining different worlds.

MALMAISON

MARTIN WISHART

RESTAURANTS

The Raj on the Shore (F D3)
→ 91 Henderson St, Leith
Tel. (0131) 553 3980
Sun-Thu noon–2.30pm, 5.30–11pm; Fri-Sat noon–2.30pm, 5.30pm–midnight
A genuine curry house with a splendid view of the Water of Leith and even more splendid value-for-money meals. £18.

Khublai Khan Mongolian Barbecue (F D3)
→ 43 Assembly St, Leith
Tel. (0131) 555 0005
Daily 6–11pm (also lunch Fri and Sun 12.30–2.30pm)
Claims to faithfully re-create 'the style of cooking favored by marauding 13th-century Mongolian warriors'. Though the kangaroo and springbok steaks served here must have been rather rare in the Gobi, the all-you-can-eat buffet is very popular with parties and the music is very infectious. £18.50–23.50.

Fisher's (F D2)
→ 1 The Shore, Leith
Tel. (0131) 554 5666
Mon-Sat 12.30–4pm, 6.30–10.30pm; Sun 12.30–10pm
Romantically sited under the 1685 Signal Tower, this pub-bistro prepares one of Scotland's most imaginative seafood menus. Check out the blackboard for the daily specials (the Loch Fyne oysters are fantastic). You will have to book for the bistro (as even Tony Blair does). £20–25.

Skippers (F D2)
→ 1a Dock Place, Leith
Tel. (0131) 554 1018
Daily 12.30–2pm (2.30pm Sun), 7–10pm
Another well-known, refined seafood restaurant with a somewhat quirky decor and music, but there's nothing eccentric about the food. Leave some room after the main course, as the desserts are exceptional. £25–30.

The Waterfront (F D2)
→ 1c Dock Place, Leith
Tel. (0131) 554 7427
Daily noon–10pm
Sleepy during the day, but buzzing with life in the evening, this tiny brick house on the canal is one of the most attractive pub-bistros in the city. It has patinated wood fittings, low ceilings, cozy corners, a mahogany bar and a landlord keen to reminisce. The fish dishes rival those of the nearby Skippers and Fisher's restaurants: mussels in garlic, fried squid, swordfish in olive oil,

CAFÉ TRUVA

OCEAN TERMINAL

THE LEITH FRONT

crab in basil, mackerel in a thick, cold marinade sauce and some excellent oysters. £22–27.

Malmaison Brasserie (F D2)
→ 1 Tower Place, Leith Tel. (0131) 468 5001 Mon-Fri 7–10am; Sat 8–10.30am (10am Sun), noon–2.15pm, 6–10.45pm (10.15pm Sun)
The British chain of boutique hotels is now renowned throughout the UK, but this was the very first Malmaison. The brasserie is marvelous, with a rather old-fashioned feel. For something different, try the Sunday brunch with eggs Benedict and corned beef hash. A less formal bar is adjacent. £22–25.

Martin Wishart (F D2)
→ 54 The Shore, Leith Tel. (0131) 553 3557 Tue-Fri noon–2pm, 6.45–9.30pm; Sat 6.45–9.30pm
Michelin-starred, highly popular restaurant whose reputation hasn't ceased to climb since its opening in 1999. Imaginative dishes and impeccable service. Treat yourself to the tasting menu. £40.

CAFÉS

Cafe Truva (F D2)
→ 77 The Shore, Leith

Tel. (0131) 554 5502 Daily 9am–6.30pm
Highly popular Turkish café serving classic summery Turkish food: healthy, affordable and tasty, with sweet desserts such as baklavas.

BARS

Bar Java (F D3)
→ 48-50 Constitution St, Leith Tel. (0131) 467 7527 Mon-Wed 7am–midnight (Thu-Fri 1am); Sat-Sun 8am–midnight
Well-liked hotel bar in an area where many pubs can seem a bit intimidating late on – good honest food and a pleasant wee beer garden.

Carriers Quarters (F D3)
→ 42 Bernard St, Leith Tel. (0131) 554 4122 Daily 11am–1am
An English-style (and none the worse for that) real-ale pub dating back to the 18th century. Friendly atmosphere; the folk music sessions on Thursdays are popular and cheery affairs.

The King's Wark (F D2)
→ 36 The Shore, Leith Tel. (0131) 554 9260 Sun-Thu noon–11pm (11am Sun); Fri-Sat noon–midnight
A fine upmarket old pub in a 17th-century building

(donated by James I to innkeeper Bernard Lindsay), with good food and a relaxed ambience.

The Starbank Inn
(off map, west of F A1)
→ 64 Laverockbank Rd, Leith Tel. (0131) 552 4141 Sun-Wed 11am–11pm (11.30am Sun); Thu-Sat 11am–midnight
Rated for its fine food and even finer ales and wines, with good views from its waterfront position. The pretty conservatory is best appreciated in summer.

Port o' Leith (F D3)
→ 58 Constitution St, Leith Tel. (0131) 554 3568 Mon-Sat 9am–1am; Sun 12.30pm–1am
A very popular old-fashioned pub with no trimmings and a working-class client base. It can be great fun, but is perhaps one for the Bravehearts.

SHOPPING

Ocean Terminal (F C2)
→ Ocean Drive, Leith Tel. (0131) 555 888 Mon-Sat 10am–8pm (7pm Sat); Sun 11pm–6pm www.oceanterminal.com
As the Scottish tourist industry keeps saying, the Leith shore has moved on from that epochal film Trainspotting, and has

become a strikingly vibrant area. The transformation is symbolised by this huge shopping complex: bars, restaurants and cinema are all open until midnight.

Leith Gallery (F D2)
→ 65 The Shore, Leith Tel. (0131) 553 5255 Mon-Sat 11am–5pm (4pm Sat) www.the-leith-gallery.co.uk
A key venue for encountering the best in Scottish contemporary art; a well-run, award-winning gallery, giving friendly advice on what to buy within your budget, whether a watercolor or a silver ring.

Kinloch Anderson (F C2)
→ Commercial St / Dock St, Leith Tel. (0131) 555 1390 Mon-Sat 9am–5.30pm www.kinlochanderson.com
One of the best-known outlets for Highland wear.

Leith Market (F C2)
→ Commercial Quay, Leith Sat 9am–5.30pm; Sun 10am–4pm www.leithmarket.com
Opened spring 2005, Leith market is a brand-new development: an enclosed permanent market offering a high-quality retail mix, from fashion and food to antiques and books.

PORTOBELLO

★ PORTOBELLO BEACH

PROMENADE

LANG TER
PICHO TER
ABERCORN TER
ABERCORN PARK
LANG TER
PITTVILLE ST
BELLFIELD ST
BELLFIELD ST
STRATTON PL
RAMSAY LANE
REGENT ST
BATH STREET
MELVILLE AVE
FIGGATE ST
BEACH LA
PIPE ST
BRIDGE ST
PORTOBELLO TOWER
WEST BANK ST
WESTBANK ST

HIGH STREET
B6415

LEE CRES
BRIGHTON CRES
ROSEFIELD PL
ROSEFIELD AVE
ADELPHI PLS
ADELAID CRES

ROSEFIELD PARK

BAILEYFIELD ESTATE
BAILEYFIELD RD
BAILEYFIELD RD

SIR HARRY LAUDER ROAD A199

0   150 m
0   164.1 yards

ALBERT DOCK

IMPERIAL DOCK

EDINBURGH DOCK

OCEAN DRIVE

CONSTITUTION STREET
TOWER STREET

LEITH CUSTOMS HOUSE ★
SHORE

ALBERT ROAD
BATH RD
SALT
BALTIC ST
BATH ST
BERNARD ST
ASSEMBLY ST
CADIZ ST
MARITIME ST
MITCHELL ST

LAMB'S HOUSE ★

QUEEN
WATER
SOUTH
ZESS

2

1

F   E   D

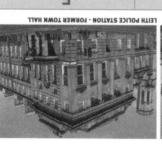

LEITH POLICE STATION - FORMER TOWN HALL

ST MARGARET'S CHURCH

Lothian bus routes in Edinbur

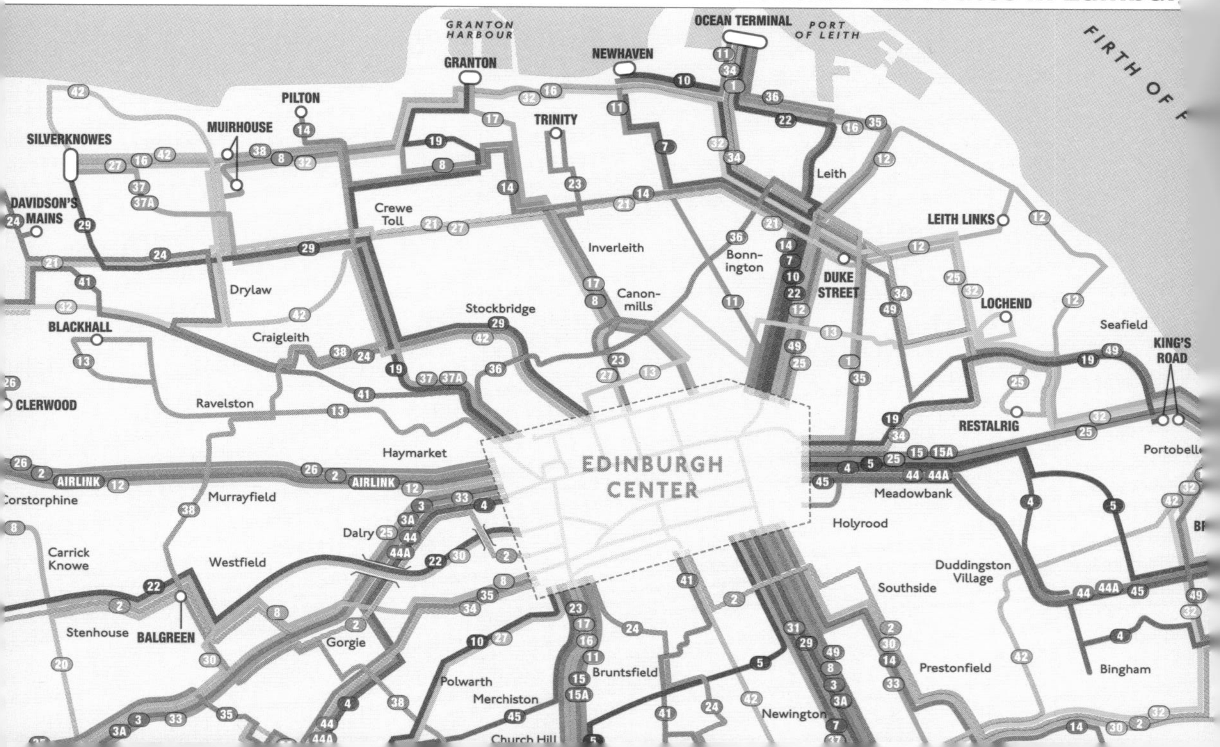

PUB LIFE

Edinburgh Airport
8 miles west of the city.
Tel. 0870 040 0007
To the city center
By taxi: around 25 mins.
Average price £15–20.
By Express Bus n° 100:
Outside Arrival Hall. Daily,
24 hrs a day; £3 one-way.
Terminates at Waverley
Bridge, near the main
railway station (**A** D1)

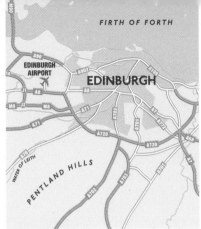

FLYING TO EDINBURGH

THE USA

There are no direct flights
to Edinburgh but regular
ones from New York,
Chicago and Los Angeles
via London or Amsterdam.
United
Tel. 1 800 538 2929
www.united.com
British Airways
Tel. 1 800 AIRWAYS
www.ba.com
Virgin Atlantic
Tel. 1 800 862 8621
www.virgin-atlantic.com
KLM
Tel. 1 800 447 4747
www.klm.com
Other websites
www.travelocity.com
www.orbitz.com

*Unless otherwise indicated,
the following prices refer to a
double room with en-suite
bathroom in low and high
season, including breakfast.
Make sure you reserve ahead
for accommodation during
the Edinburgh Festival.*

UNDER £100

MW Guesthouse (D B4)
➔ *94 Dalkeith Rd, Newington
Tel. (0131) 662 9265
www.mwguesthouse.co.uk*
A sleek and centrally
located guest house with
modern decor in shades of
brown and cream. Six
rooms (all en-suite), and
most with glorious views
over Arthur's Seat and the
Salisbury Crags. From £40
to £110, depending on the
season and room.
Ailsa Craig Hotel (D A1)
➔ *24 Royal Terrace
Tel. (0131) 556 6055/1022
ailsacraighotel@ednet.co.uk*
Designed by William

Playfair and dating from
1820, this elegant house is
only a 15-minute walk away
from Princes St. It's
perhaps on the shabby-
genteel side, but it is
nevertheless good value.
Sixteen rooms: £50–90.
Ben Doran Guest House
(off map, 100 yards south
of **D** A4)
➔ *11 Mayfield Gardens
Tel. (0131) 667 8488
www.ben-doran.co.uk*
A fine Georgian house with
11 rooms and excellent
views, southeast of the
Meadows and a short walk
from the city center.
Traditional Scottish but
vegetarian-friendly food,
and quality service all
round. From £50 to £60
depending on whether
room has en-suite bath.
**Travelodge Edinburgh
Central (B** B3)
➔ *33 St Mary's St
Tel. 0870 191 1637
www.travelodge.co.uk*

There are two other
Travelodges near
Edinburgh center, all no-
frills and helpful staff. The
hotel itself (a modern
construction) is not a pretty
sight, but as it is 100 yards
from the Royal Mile and
you're only here to sleep
this is exceptional value.
Standard amenities in the
spotless rooms (en-suite
bathroom, TV, tea/coffee-
making facilities...).
From £55 a night.
Premier Travel Inn (A B4)
➔ *82 Lauriston Place
Tel. 0870 9906610
www.premiertravelinn.com*
Like the Travelodges, the
Travel Inns are comfortable,
no-nonsense stop-overs;
has an integral bar and
restaurant, but unless
you're very lazy, eat
somewhere else (the
much-more exciting
Grassmarket is just round
the corner). There are two
other Travel Inns in

Edinburgh: friendly and
value for money. From
£62 a night.
Greenside Hotel (D A1)
➔ *9 Royal Terrace
Tel. (0131) 557 0022*
Another old-style hotel in
the Playfair-designed Royal
Terrace (see Ailsa Craig
Hotel), the Greenside gets
good word-of-mouth
recommendation. Fifteen
rooms, all with the usual
amenities: colour TV, radio,
tea/coffee-making
facilities, hairdryer and
telephone. £60–90.
**Ceilidh-Donia
Hotel (D** B4)
➔ *14-16 Marchhall Crescent
Tel. 0131 667 2743
www.hotelceilidh-donia.co.uk*
Despite the hotel's bizarre
claim to be Edinburgh's
answer to the 'Hotel
California', this is a very
fine small hotel. It caters for
special diets, has a ground-
floor room with wheelchair-
access, and welcome

HOLYROOD PALACE FROM CALTON HILL

TRAVELING BY TRAIN

From London
From London King's Cross, trains leave every hour for Edinburgh (4 ⅓ hrs) and Glasgow (5 hrs). Tickets from £60 return.
National Rail Enquiries
Tel. 0845 748 4950
www.gner.co.uk
Scot Rail
Tel. 0845 755 0033
www.scotrail.co.uk
Waverley Station
Edinburgh's main railway station is in the city center and can be reached by taxi or bus. From here there are services to Glasgow and a variety of other destinations in Scotland and England. Most train services also operate from Edinburgh Haymarket station which is on the main bus route between the airport and city center.
Further information:
Tel. 0845 748 4950
www.travelinescotland.com

TRAVELING BY BUS

A practical way to travel. Two companies are competing for the privilege of ferrying you throughout the city and its surroundings areas: Lothian Buses (see map p. 29) and First Edinburgh
Lothian Buses
31 Waverley Bridge
Tel. (0131) 555 6363
www.lothianbuses.co.uk
Have the exact fare ready. 1-day bus card is £2.30.
First Edinburgh
Tel. 08708 72 72 71
www.firstgroup.com
1-day bus card £2.30–8 depending on the zone.

extras such as DVD players and broadband in every room. Movies are on loan from reception. It is ten minutes by taxi from the center. Sixteen rooms: from £60 to £140 depending on the season.

Castle Guest House (A D2**)**
→ 38 Castle Street
www.castleguesthouse.com
Tel. (0131) 225 1975
On the top two floors (no elevator) of a Georgian town house right in the center of town, the renovated Castle Guest House offers seven rooms, all with en-suite shower rooms, TV, hairdryer and tea/coffee-making facilities. Non-smoking throughout. £60–£80 depending on season (hearty breakfast incl.). A few doors down, at no. 30 is the **Castle View Guest House**, a four-star guest house similar to the one above. £70–£120 depending on the season.
Tel. (0131) 226 5784
www.castleviewgh.co.uk

The Inverleith Hotel (C B2**)**
→ 5 Inverleith Terrace
Tel. (0131) 556 2745
www.inverleithhotel.co.uk
A 15-minute walk from the city center. Beside the wondrous Botanic Garden this fine establishment is real value for money. The building itself is a first-rate example of an early Victorian town house. Ten bedrooms, of which one has a four-poster bed. £60–£120 depending on season and room. Also available is a self-catering apartment for five to seven people (£90–160 a night).

Haymarket & Buchan Hotel (E C2**)**
→ 1 Coates Gardens
Tel. (0131) 337 1775
www.haymarket-hotel.co.uk
Family-run, family-friendly and near to Haymarket station, this fine Victorian hotel makes a great base for seeing West Edinburgh. Smart rooms for up to four people with a fair number of options. The 25 rooms have en-suite shower, except one with en-suite bath. Doubles £60–100.

53 Frederick Street (C C5**)**
53 Frederick Street
Tel. (0131) 226 2752
www.53frederickstreet.com
A Georgian town house situated in the heart of the New Town and a stone's throw from the pubs of Rose Street. All the stylishly furnished rooms have en-suite shower, DVD player and tea/coffee-making facilities. £80–£130 depending on season.

Newington Cottage (D B4**)**
→ 15 Blacket Place
Tel. (0131) 668 1935
www.newcot.demon.co.uk
One mile south from the

NEWHAVEN HERITAGE MUSEUM

SOUTH LEITH PARISH CHURCH

k (5–11 June,
.leithfestival.com), take
ntage of the station
day to examine the
ing's chambers and
– but do resist the
station to recite the old
ue-twister 'The Leith
e Dismisseth us...'
ity House (F D3)
rkgate
0131) 554 3289
historic-scotland.gov.uk
gned by Thomas Brown,
classical Georgian
e was constructed for
ncorporation of
hers and Ship's Masters
16–18 (replacing one
55); it contains many
nating relics of Leith's

maritime heritage. Take a
guided tour and see the
stunning stained-glass
window over the stairway.
Portobello Beach (F F1)
➔ *www.portobello-
edinburgh.org.uk*
Portobello is Edinburgh's
seaside resort. The mile-
long beach is clean and
sandy, but the seafront
facing it is, alas, café-less,
amenity-free and dispiriting.
Even the amazing octagonal
tower (built in 1785 from
reclaimed stone from the
Old Town) is encircled by
an 'entertainment' gallery.
Sir Harry Lauder, the
archetypal Scot before Billy
Connolly broke the mold,

was born in Portobello at
4 Bridge St in 1870.
**Leith Customs
House (F** D2)
➔ *Commercial Street*
Built by Robert Reid in
1810–12, this massive
Doric-style building – where
ship masters would declare
cargos and pay duty – is
used by the National
Museum of Scotland as a
store and is unfortunately
closed to the public.
**Newhaven Heritage
Museum (F** A1)
➔ *24 Pier Place*
Tel. (0131) 551 4165
Daily 9am–4.30pm
The fishing boats have long
gone from this port, but this

excellent small museum
brings a lost way of life
back; the 'dressing up' box
is very popular with kids.
**South Leith Parish
Church (F** D3)
➔ *Kirkgate*
Tel. (0131) 554 2578
www.slpc.co.uk
Though the current
building was erected by
Thomas Hamilton in 1848,
the church's core dates to
1487, and has especial
appeal to fans of *The Da
Vinci Code* (*see also
Excursions*) with the many
templar legends and often
bloody history associated
with the site; it has a lively
congregation.

Street names, monuments and pl...

references following each entry allow you to situate it in one or more of the six geographical areas presented in the guide.

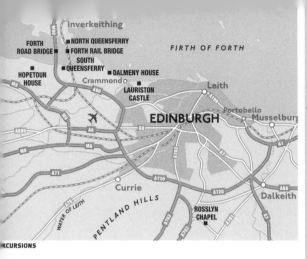

occasional very interesting last-minute special offers.

OVER £150

The Howard (C C4)
→ 34 Great King St
Tel. (0131) 557 3500
www.thehoward.com
This elegant and discreet five-star hotel occupies three 18th-century houses in a splendid location. Eighteen spacious, individually decorated rooms with all amenities and very attentive service. There's an excellent restaurant, the Atholl. And if you can't stay here why not come for a traditional Scottish afternoon tea – cakes, scones and jams, finger sandwiches for £12.95 per person. Reserve. £198–296.

The Scotsman (B A2)
→ 20 North Bridge
Tel. (0131) 556 5565
www.thescotsmanhotel.co.uk

Former home of *The Scotsman* newspaper, this magnificent building, an opulent example of English Baroque (1899–1902), has now been transformed into a stylish five-star hotel. It is set close to the center and overlooks Princes St Gardens. There is an emphasis on marble in the interior decor, with wood paneling stencilled with the names of former editors. The 56 rooms all slightly vary, with contemporary artwork and tweeds from the Scottish estates. All have widescreen TV, DVD and computer with internet access. The restaurant and brasserie serve modern Scottish cuisine, while in the bar, cases containing 399 types of whisky line the walls. From £250.

The Caledonian Hilton (A A2)
→ Princes St
Tel. (0131) 222 8888

www.hilton.com
This huge Edwardian block of red sandstone (1903), affectionately known as the 'Caley', was taken over in 2000 by the Hilton chain and had a £6.4 million makeover last year, with two restaurants and a bar. Standing at the western end of Princes St it remains Edinburgh's most famous hotel, with 233 rooms and 13 suites. From £245.

The Balmoral (B A2)
→ 1 Princes St
Tel. (0131) 556 2414
www.thebalmoralhotel.com
This luxury hotel dominates the eastern end of Princes St. The bedrooms, whose re-decoration was overseen by Olga Polizzi in 2004, are superb. There's a fitness center, a swimming pool and two very good restaurants: Number One and Hadrian's. It has 188 rooms and 8 suites; doubles from £240.

in flannel and burdock burrs in early August, may give the unwary a start. The custom was first recorded in the 17th century.

Dalmeny House
→ Take A90 Forth Bridge Rd from Edinburgh
Tel. (0131) 331 1888
July-Aug, Sun-Tue: house & tearoom open 2–5.30pm
www.dalmeny.co.uk
The family home of the Earls of Rosebery, it was built in the Tudor Revival style by William Wilkins in 1817 and houses many fine paintings and objects. Dalmeny Village itself is a conservation area with a 12th-century church.

Hopetoun House
→ South Queensferry
Take A90 Forth Road Bridge Road from Edinburgh to slip road just outside village
Tel. (0131) 319 1885 March 25-Sep 25: daily 10am–5.30pm
More of a palace than a house, this seat of the Earls of Hopetoun is set in 150 acres of parkland and was built in 1699 by Sir William Bruce (finished by William Adam in 1748). The interior is exquisitely furnished in exemplary Georgian mode.

Lauriston Castle
→ Cramond Road South
Tel. (0131) 336 2060
April-Oct: Sat-Thu: guided tours hourly 11.20am–4.20pm. Nov-March: Sat-Sun 2.20 & 3.20pm; grounds open 9am–dusk
This 1590s tower house may evoke its warlike past, but inside it is a beautifully preserved Edwardian mansion. Visit the 18th-century village of Cramond, with its Roman remains; the Cramond Lioness, an 1,800-year-old sculpture, was found here in 1997.

ORTH RAIL BRIDGE

ORTH ROAD BRIDGE

STOCKBRIDGE

ty center, built in yellow
andstones on a classical
alian design with a
olonnaded porch,
ewington Cottage is an
xceptional guest house. It
only has three rooms –
uiet, comfortable and
pacious – so book early.
90–110.

100–150

llison House Hotel
off map, 100 yards south
D A4)
➜ 17 Mayfield Gardens
el. 0800 328 9003
ww.allisonhousehotel.com
amily-run, 11-bedroomed,
egantly decorated guest
ouse south of the center
n Newington and about
5 minutes by bus from the
oyal Mile. £100.

unstane House
otel (E B2)
➜ 4 West Coates
el. (0131) 337 6169
ww. dunstane-hotel-
edinburgh.co.uk
Near the Haymarket
station, this charming and
comfortable Victorian
house is basically a four-
star hotel with three-star
prices. Throw in a highly
rated restaurant, Skerries,
and you've got a fabulous
place to stay. Sixteen
rooms; £100–140.

Malmaison (F D2)
➜ 1 Tower Place, Leith
Tel. (0131) 468 5000
www.malmaison.com
The first Malmaison is a
former seamen's mission
(1833) near the docks with
impressive 'designer'
decor, relaxed service and
French-style brasserie
serving good, simply
prepared food. It has a gym
and internet access in all
rooms. Reservations over
the Internet are cheaper.
100 rooms, from £135.

The Bonham (E C-D1)
➜ 33-35 Drumsheugh Gdns
Tel. (0131) 226 6050

www.thebonham.com
First opened in 1988, this
modern 'boutique' hotel
consists of three small
buildings overlooking a
peaceful, green square.
The 48 rooms are bright,
comfortable and attractive,
but the bathrooms are
rather small. Excellent
restaurant. £135–195.

Channings (E C1)
➜ 12–16 South Learmonth
Gardens, Comely Bank
Tel. (0131) 274 7401
www.channings.co.uk
Five, four-story terraced
houses (1900) form this
charming club-hotel. Cozy
and comfortably furnished,
with several stunningly
modern rooms, three
gardens and a patio.
The hotel also boasts one
of Edinburgh's finest
restaurants, Channings
(see **E**), and a meal here is
recommended. 48 rooms,
2 suites; standard double
£138–185. Sometimes

Rosslyn Chapel
➜ Take A701 road from
Edinburgh to Roslin village
Tel. (0131) 440 2159
Mon-Sat 10am–5pm;
Sun noon–4.4pm
www.rosslynchapel.org.uk
Visitors must note that
Rosslyn, made famous by
The Da Vinci Code, is a
working episcopal church.
Founded by Sir William St
Clair in 1446, Rosslyn has
always been seen as
unusual, indeed unique in
what the antiquary John
Britton called its 'variety
and eccentricity'. The
interior suffered badly in
the Reformation, but much
of its wonders remained,
such as the roof and the
'Apprentice Pillar'.

Forth Rail and
Road bridges
➜ South Queensferry
Take A90 Forth Bridge Road
from Edinburgh
www.forthbridges.org.uk
Arguably one of the finest
engineering feats in the
world, the Forth Rail Bridge
spans 1,710 ft and became
the world's first major steel
bridge in 1899 (63 men
died in its construction).
The Road Bridge was
opened in 1964 and is one
of the longest suspension
bridges in Europe.

The South Queensferry
Museum
➜ 53 High St, South
Queensferry
Tel. (0131) 331 5545
Mon, Thu-Sat 10am–1pm;
Sun noon–5pm
Offers fine views of the
Forth and the history of
Queensferry and Dalmeny.
The life-size model of the
ancient 'Burry Man', in
which a local is decked out